From HUMAN DOING to HUMAN BEING

Getting Back to Basics and Tuning into Yourself Again

TASH JARVIS

Disclaimer:
All information shared in this book is done so with positive intentions, and whilst intended to inform, this work is not intended as a substitute for professional advice. If you find that you have difficulty letting go of fearful thoughts, or that they are impacting your life negatively, please contact a medical professional.

From Human Doing to Human Being: Getting Back to Basics and Tuning into Yourself Again
© Tash Jarvis 2021

ISBN: 978-1-922532-39-8 (Paperback)
          978-1-922532-40-4 (eBook)

A catalogue record for this book is available from the National Library of Australia

Cover Design: Ocean Reeve Publishing
Design and Typeset: Ocean Reeve Publishing
Printed in Australia by Ocean Reeve Publishing

Published by Tash Jarvis and Ocean Reeve Publishing

www.oceanreevepublishing.com

Dedicated to Jesse.

Thank you for encouraging me to write this book.
Without you, it would still be just a dream of mine.

PREFACE

Whether you have just begun your self-development journey or have been on it for some time, it is important to trust the process. It is my hope that the ideas in this book will resonate with you and give you some guidance as to how to bring about change in order to live a deeper, more meaningful life. As magical as it would be for a book to solve all your problems and tell you how to live the rest of your life, it simply isn't possible. While I don't have any secrets to reveal about what your future looks like, I will provide titbits, tips, and strategies to help you create the future you want.

Many of us live on the surface, and what I mean by that is we go our whole lives without seeing what we are fully capable of. We choose to stay in our comfort zones, meaning we live in a place where everything is known, and we feel we are in control of our lives for the most part. This is one of life's greatest tragedies because not only do you miss out on discovering your greatest gift, but the world also misses out. When you are feeling fearful or doubtful, remember that good things come from growth zones. It's in the moments when we try something new or find a new part of ourselves that we find the magic. For those who have lain on their death bed, living a life that was less than what they had desired can be one of their biggest regrets. Instead of waiting for the perfect time, try now. You don't need to have it all figured out to begin.

Be grateful for being alive and that you have the opportunity to be proactive and make changes now that can lead you to your best life and become your best self. You can choose to live the same year over and over or you can follow your intuition, run your own race, and live a meaningful and magical life which allows you to grow. Live deeply. Be authentic and choose to evolve rather than settle.

You may feel obligated to live your life on others' terms, following the advice of loved ones or strangers. While following this advice may not seem harmful, you may end up supressing your own visions for how you wish to lead your life. Your creativity is hidden, dreams are buried, and for a while, you live on the surface. You can convince yourself that you are happy and you don't need more from life, but then there is the burning feeling inside you that makes you feel uneasy. It is reminding you what you are truly capable of. It's your wake-up call.

You begin to evaluate where you are in life and if you are heading in the direction that you want to go. When you notice this feeling, lean into the curiosity. Try something new; challenge yourself and monitor the outcome. There is no one-size-fits-all approach to a personal development journey. Each journey is different, and what works for someone else may not work for you. If that happens, trust yourself enough to let it go and try something else until you find what works for you.

If we seek validation and measure our success by external sources, we may never be at peace with our inner self. If we want to achieve true peace, we must begin with self-love, identifying what you want to give and receive from life, and determining whether you want to reset parts of your life to build a life you are capable of living.

My biggest fear is the notion of settling. I am not perfect; I have passed up opportunities and made choices based on the ease or safeness of it rather than saying yes to what I truly wanted, and I have to live with those decisions. With that being said, I followed my heart by going on a six-month working holiday to Canada and that has been one of my biggest adventures to date. Those six months of collective moments are something that I won't forget because it was the first time in so long that I had said yes to myself and silenced the voices of those around me. It wasn't to be mean; I simply knew what I wanted to do and I wasn't prepared to let anyone else talk me out of going. It was a defining chapter in my life, and I am grateful that I was brave enough to say yes to myself even though it meant being away from family and friends for a while and not knowing if I'd enjoy living overseas or not. Just remember, there will always be naysayers, and while they may mean well, you have the power to decide whose words you listen to. The rest is merely white noise.

When you open yourself up to new experiences, you grow. You begin to break the loop of sameness by welcoming newness into your life. Granted, the growth isn't always pain-free. There are always growing pains such as perceived failure which brings knowledge, and with achievement comes motivation. If we want to lead meaningful lives and contribute all that we are capable of, we must be our authentic selves and live the life we want to lead rather than following a script that others are writing for us, well-intentioned or not.

You can ask others for guidance, be bold and try new things, read books, attend workshops, and find like-minded people who can support you to become the best version of yourself. Such options can help fuel your inspiration and provide guidance when you need it, but it is only the beginning. There is so much more to your journey. Change must come from within; we cannot expect others to change our lives for us. You need to empower yourself to make decisions, to strive to be better than who you were previously and be willing to learn and grow.

Life is complex. As children, we are encouraged to dream big and free. In our innocence, our minds know no barriers; it is only when we grow up and live to see more sunrises and sunsets that we begin to place a ceiling on our own abilities. We are limited by the stories we tell ourselves. If you want something, work for it. You may not always get the outcome you were hoping for, but use those times as lessons and keep going. If you've picked up a copy of this book, then you are different, you are willing to do the work to learn about yourself, your skills and habits, and how to build on these to create a richer life.

We are all capable of more than we believe. When we become too complacent, we live within the boundaries of our comfort zones. We stick to our routines and then we find ourselves wondering what happened to us. The days are long, but the years are short. When you live the same year over again, time will pass in the blink of an eye. We may get into a serious relationship, start a family or new job, and suddenly we become a shadow of our former self. During these times, self-care can get pushed aside as you are taking care of others, too busy focusing on seemingly urgent tasks that are taxing your time and energy, and what made you *you* is no longer present in your life.

I believe we all have a gift inside us; some wake up knowing how they want to spend their lives, while many of us aren't sure. We fall into habits and jobs that aren't meant for us and we just accept that this is the reality. We can change our circumstances if we so choose. You can take control of your life and adopt practices to help you get from where you are to where you want to be.

It isn't going to be easy, but you are worth it. You deserve to live, not just exist.

You are worthy; you have a story to write and share. Live life with determination and gratitude rather than in fear. Be your own advocate rather than toughest critic. It isn't easy to live a life that is true to yourself. We can often feel like we are obligated to live a life that is deemed suitable by our parents, friends, family, or society. What happens when you try to run someone else's race? You will never win. If you want to win a race, run your own race.

As a millennial, I grew up when mobile phones were bricks—before flip phones were all the rage; when you had to wait for a modem to connect to the internet and *Friends* was still showing on TV. Now life is a little more fast-paced, and while technology can help us connect on a more global scale and in an instant, it also shows the need for introspection and finding who you are.

I've had a hunger in my stomach for a number of years and so I embarked on the quest of self-discovery. One of the greatest realisations I have had on this journey so far is that if we seek gratification and acceptance from external sources, we will never be happy or at peace with ourselves. When we focus on the attainment of materialistic items at the expense of meaningful relationships, our values, or pursuing a life that has a purpose, we feel empty.

When you live a life not meant for you—which goes against your values, beliefs, and what brings you true joy— you will experience a disconnect between yourself and your soul. There is a void, a sense of inner calm longing to be discovered. Grow into the person you were destined to become rather than a shadow of your potential.

My hope for this book is to remind you that you are capable of achieving all that you want and you can transform into the person you were meant to become. It is not an overnight fix; you may need to discover those deep-planted habits, evaluate who you allow to use your time, energy, and money, and ask yourself a few big questions that we so often we sweep under the rug. It is possible.

Many books I have read are from the perspective of those who have completed their initial transformation and are thriving in their lives. I genuinely believe that no life is perfect regardless of the highlight reels we see on various social media platforms. We all want to lead lives that we are proud of. If we can live life according to our values, are able to use our strengths, and connect on a deeper level with others, that's when we can find peace and happiness.

I have written this book as a guide with tips and some personal stories within it. I hope some of the tips resonate with you and that you can implement them into your life and see results. It may not be immediate; this is not a fad guide where you'll be a millionaire in two days, nor will your life flip 180 degrees in a matter of weeks. It is a guide on how to lead a life filled with meaning and purpose, where every day can be a highlight reel. Revel in the little moments; be grateful and joyous. The energy you put out into the world will come back to you. Aim to live at a higher frequency; if we begin a moment of mindful living, connecting to our spirituality and transforming into our best selves, the world will be a better place because of it.

CONTENTS

INTRODUCTION

You matter. You have been created for a purpose and you deserve to be the best version of yourself that you can be. You have a unique story to write and discover. Whether you believe in a higher being, the universe, destiny, fate, or none of these, each of us is here for a reason.

Some may live their whole life without questioning their existence or their 'why'. While this may result in a happy existence, such individuals are living on the surface. Living on the surface occurs when we simply exist—when we don't take time to look inward or learn about ourselves and others. While there is no right or wrong way to live life, looking inward allows us to discover more about who we are and why we do what we do. It helps us to identify our blind spots, triggers, and ideologies that drive the ways we think, work, and play. Self-growth and personal development is not always a smooth-sailing journey; it takes introspection, grit, and patience. Others experience a burning feeling inside, the yearning for something more, and want to make incremental improvements in their life to reach their greatest potential.

Some may suppress this feeling and simply wish for it to go away and opt for a safe life in which they settle, choosing comfort and routine over experience and growth. Others use this feeling as a sign that they are on the path to finding out what a life well-lived looks like for them. They follow this intuition, digging deep within themselves, searching for knowledge through trial and error, and create a life of their design. The question is: which statement resonates with you?

The possibilities are endless, whether we choose to live life or merely exist is our own choice. Our decisions shape our lives, and it is up to you what life you choose to create. We can choose to be grateful for what we have and who we are and who we are becoming or we can choose to be blind, to play it safe, and believe that this is all there is. Settling can lead to resentment and regret. If you choose to live in your growth zone and continue to grow, it doesn't mean you'll have a challenge-free life. It does mean that you get to see what you are capable of; you can answer the 'what-ifs' with actions and know the outcome when you try something new.

Revel in beginnings and learning something new. Remember, all masters started as apprentices. Growth requires learning, trying, and challenging yourself, and through this messy yet beautiful journey, we get better. In the digital age, we are exposed to highlight reels on our social media feeds. Our insecurities lead us to begin to believe that we are not like the others, nor can we reach high levels of success in any (or all) areas of our life. It is not an impossible feat, but it is not an easy road either. There are no shortcuts to success; you must hold yourself accountable, learn from challenges, and be resilient in the face of adversity and challenge. Life was never designed to be easy nor are two lives identical.

Many of us are scared to be vulnerable or be our authentic selves for fear of judgement. We would rather play it small than take a risk and lose our pride. Being vulnerable and having faith is daunting because it requires doing your best while relying on variables outside of your control and hoping for the outcome that you desire. It means tuning into your heart rather than listening to your head if it's filled with an inflated sense of self-importance. Decisions made based solely from a place of self-importance may not achieve the best results. It can also block you from asking for help or looking at situations from a different perspective. A life of depth offers many treasures if you are courageous enough to try.

When we act from a place of self-importance, pride gets in the way. When we choose to tune into our heart and act with grace, we act with kindness. If you are used to living life with your ego, it takes work to tune back into your heart. Rather than asking the universe 'Why has this happened to me?' why not ask a different question? Ask yourself, 'Why is this happening *for* me?', 'What lesson is it here to teach me?' Notice the way each sentence makes you feel. The first sentence is ego-based; you are focusing on the situation rather than the solution. The second sentence is powerful because instead of thinking with a victim mindset, you are looking for solutions, a positive, and a lesson to be learned.

Each journey is different, so in times when comparison takes over, reflect on Jon Acuff's quote: 'Never compare your beginning to someone else's middle.'[1]

I have chosen to write this book with short chapters. That way, you can spend a few minutes reading and reflecting on the words. Any personal development tool such as this book and other learning materials offer a wealth of knowledge, but it is only part of the inner work you need to do. This book provides guidance, but it does not mean that once you read it cover to cover that your life will be instantly transformed and your worries go away. It simply means you know better so you can do better.

Chapter 1

WRITE YOUR OWN STORY

It's time to begin again by reclaiming your power. Grab a pen and write your own story. Be brave enough to block out the noise and focus on you—your wants, needs, values, and dreams. You are worthy of living a life on your terms and to strive for your dreams rather than settling or playing it small.

It's easy to get caught up in the crowd by going through the motions and ticking off items on the list society dictates. The list might include things such as choosing a career that offers a good salary, finding ways to fit in with others if you're prone to standing out, saying yes to please others, and settling down to start a family. As young children, many of us are told to go to school, get an education, and when you're done, either get a job or further your education by attending TAFE, university, or college—even if you're unsure about what you want to do. We are encouraged to decide how we would like to spend our lives when we are still in school. Some may know what their calling is, but for the majority, we aren't sure. We don't really know what jobs exist or what we would like to fill our workdays with.

Then once you are an adult, you are conditioned to get a well-paying job, pay your bills, and then find a partner to settle down with and have children. It is as if your story has already been written with the chapters set out, the only thing missing is the timeline for when these events occur in your life. Now, not everyone follows the checklist, but those who don't follow the status quo may feel pressure or guilt. I often think that the trailblazers are some of the bravest people, as they have the courage to follow their dreams rather than being limited by others.

We are all unique, yet we seem to try to fit a mould, even when it doesn't feel right. As a result, we are willing to make sacrifices just to belong to a community, place, or organisation which we don't really want to be a part of in the first place. It's emotionally taxing to pretend to be someone you aren't.

If you want to find peace within yourself, stay true to who you are. Once you discover your values, ideologies you live by, and who you want to be in life, stand by it. If you choose to show your true self, some may leave, but rather than perceiving it as a loss, accept that you are now making room for people who will treasure you for who you truly are rather than what they expect you to be. You get one life; live it on your terms.

When you have settled or are living a smaller life than you may want, it often takes a tragedy to wake you up from the way in which you are currently living your life. It shouldn't take a tragedy to make us reflect on the life we are living or settling for. It's time to reflect on your journey and where you want to go moving forward.

The issue with this kind of mindset is that you are simply living the same day over and over again. If you can, imagine yourself forty years from now. What do you see when you reflect on your life? What have you achieved? I'd like to think that few of us envision the same year lived seventy-five times over. Instead, I think we would envision a diverse life that was filled with different chapters, experiences, highs, and lows.

If you're discontent with where your life is heading, take action and make changes. Change starts with you. As Joe Dispenza writes in *Breaking the Habit of Being Yourself*, 'your personality reflects your personal reality'.[2] External change starts from within. When you are living a life that is not meant for you, it is hard to find inner peace. There is a yearning for more, an unsettling feeling that stems from this misalignment. Do the work, make changes, and begin to fill the void. It's freeing to be yourself rather than a version of yourself that you think others will value more.

Don't be afraid of listening to your heart rather than just your head. Too often we listen to our mind and suppress what we feel intuitively. We allow ourselves to become a victim of our circumstances by using loopholes as the reasons for why we are stuck. We make excuses by blaming external factors such as time, the economy, our relationships, education, living arrangements, or job commitments, rather than holding ourselves accountable. While not everything is within our control, we give away all our power when we play the victim. We lose our account-ability, and in turn, our ability to write our own stories. We have the power to change our circumstances if we wish to. You can live the life you want if you just begin.

It's a choice to stay or move on to something new. Either way, you must live with the consequences of your actions. Change is never easy; our minds crave comfort and sameness, but to grow means to expand. Try new things until you find habits that resonate for you. Find a job that aligns with your values rather than compromising them, a partner who loves you in spite of your imperfections, and loved ones who see the real you rather than trying to change you to suit the person they think you should be. Remember, this goes both ways: to attract such beautiful souls into your life, you need to treat others this way. Uplift, support, and inspire others so you can attract this back to you in time.

Ask yourself:

1. Do you feel like you are in control of your life?
2. Do you feel helpless?
3. What elements of your life do you feel like you have the least control?
4. How could you begin to regain control?

Chapter 2

STEPPING OUT OF YOUR COMFORT ZONE

Habits and routines can be grounding, but they also have the potential to make us complacent. When we get accustomed to existing solely in our comfort zone, we are merely existing and playing it safe. Instead, try to venture out of your comfort zone and be open to growth. Everything we find easy now we once found challenging to some degree.

According to the *Oxford Dictionary*, comfort zones are a psychological state in which we feel at ease, safe, and know what we are doing. We can do things on autopilot— that is, without much thought. Our 'growth zone', however, is filled with unknowns, newness, and makes us feel a little discomfort because we are in a learning state.

Newness can be intimidating, especially if you like to be in control; however, it allows us to build new skills and learn more. When you learn, you grow. When you fail, you grow. When you succeed, you grow. Whatever the outcome, when you step out and try something new, you gain experience and knowledge.

Trust yourself and know your worth. Growth isn't always easy. It can be messy, overwhelming, and challenging, but therein lies the reward. When you push yourself, you get to see what you are made of and we are capable of so much more than we perceive we are. Sure, there are steep learning curves at times, but if you can remind yourself that it's not about winning or losing, it's about learning, then you'll keep going. Be resilient and be open to learning from your experiences. It is through experience that we gain knowledge and wisdom. Allow life to be your teacher and you will be rewarded with valuable lessons.

Playing it safe doesn't guarantee a happy life. Standing still doesn't protect you from the highs and lows of life, but it does limit your ability to thrive and flourish. Whatever we choose—comfort or growth—time still passes. Just because we choose to stand still does not mean that time will follow our lead. We will age, others will grow and develop, and it's our choice whether we stunt our growth or facilitate it.

Take a moment to think of your future. Do you see yourself living the same year on repeat, following the same patterns and routines? Do you see something else? You are doing yourself a disservice if you choose to settle for a life that is less than what you want. You have everything within you to create the life of your dreams provided you put in the work. You can settle for a mediocre life or you can give it your all—the choice is yours to make.

You need to establish what you value more: growth or comfort, newness or sameness. If you value growth over comfort, you will be able to keep challenging yourself and moving forward.

Stepping out of your comfort zone can be daunting, but it's also exciting. I still remember when I decided to live overseas in Canada for six months. I had never lived overseas before, but I did my research, found a business that helped with the visa applications, had my interview, and before I knew it, I was living in the Rocky Mountains and shovelling snow off a driveway. If I had let my fears take over, I wouldn't have gone.

If you find yourself going through the motions, look at ways to break free of the routine, even if it's for a day or two. This allows you to recharge and refocus on the present. Just as travelling allows us to value our time, our surroundings, and be grateful for each moment, so too can a break from your daily life. Whether it be going for a massage, a walk, on a road trip, to a new restaurant, or reading a new book, try to think of something which will allow you to be a little spontaneous and out of the ordinary. It's when we break free of our routine that we can turn off autopilot and tune in with ourselves again.

Step out and step up; expand your comfort zone by moving into your growth zone, and before you know, it'll become your new comfort zone.

Chapter 3

PROGRESS > PERFECTION

Striving for perfection is like chasing the pot of gold at the end of a rainbow—just when you think you're close enough to reach it, it moves out of reach again.

Voltaire, a French philosopher, once wrote 'perfect is the enemy of good.'[3] Put simply, if we spend our time trying to be a perfect person and do tasks perfectly, we get less done. More than that, we aren't able to see that good is … well … good enough.

Hal Elrod wrote, 'personal growth is about progress, not perfection.'[4] If the aim is to grow and improve, then we cannot wait for the perfect moment.

In the 1950s, physicians Meyer Friedman and RH Rosenman identified different personality types.[5] 'A-type' personalities often strive for perfection, feel the pressures of time, and may also be impatient. If someone with this type of personality is trying to write the perfect reply to an email or be the perfect person in their work and private life, it can be exhausting. It can also be paralysing. It hinders progress and simple things can take much longer than needed. Rather than striving for perfection, we can try to become 'good-enoughers'.

There have been moments in my life when I've wanted to be the perfect person. A few years ago, my partner Jesse and I hosted our first Christmas event. To ensure the event went smoothly, I researched recipes, created an event on social media so we would know how many people would be attending, and I even went to a Christmas workshop to get some tips on how to host a Christmas party and be organised. I wanted it to be perfect, and for that to happen, I said that Jesse and I would cook most of the dinner items and organise the appetisers. Not only did this cost a fair bit of money but it also put both of us under a great deal of stress. Rather than enjoying the day, we spent most of it cooking, tidying up, and arranging the table. It made me realise that trying to be the perfect host wasn't worth the stress.

I learnt that it's okay to let others bring food to an event and that people are happy just spending time together. They're not going to be fussed if I didn't perfectly vacuum the house or if the Christmas tree ornaments weren't all colour-coded.

If you spend your life chasing perfection, you won't know true peace. If you are continuously waiting for the right time, the perfect job, person, house, or lifestyle, it will lead to disappointment. Why? Because you'll never be truly satisfied with what you have and what you've achieved, and it can block your creative spark. Allow yourself to be a novice; accept that the perfect time doesn't exist and that doing your best in that moment is all you can ask for. Perfection is not attainable.

Perfectionism may seem like the ideal trait to guarantee success, but more often than not, it hinders it. You become stuck where you are, often investing more time and energy than required. If you are a perfectionist, I would encourage you to begin to change your mindset to strive for progress rather than perfection. Learn when it is time to let go and accept that you have done all that you can. It is not an overnight fix; it will take work. Give yourself permission to accept that good is good enough.

You may be putting off tasks until the perfect time, but in reality, the perfect time does not exist. Now is the only time that is guaranteed, so begin today. Taking action and making progress will yield a greater result than waiting for the perfect time and not taking any action.

Perfectionism hinders progress and performance. It is time to change the goal posts. Strive for progress and doing your best with the resources you have available to you at that moment. When you look back in hindsight, you may feel like you could have done better, but if that was the best you could have done in the moment, let it be. If you look at world-class leaders and others who have reached high levels of success, it took time to become who they are. We don't see the hours of hard work, the learnings, the challenges, or the beginnings of their journeys. They didn't know all the answers; they asked for help and learned as they went along. You can learn as you go rather than learning it all before you begin.

Perfectionism leaves you feeling discontent, dissatisfied, and trying to fix what is not broken. We are not perfect beings, and once we learn to accept our flaws, we can free ourselves. Love yourself and others despite flaws (perceived or real). Focus on utilising your strengths rather than magnifying your weaknesses. Find others who complement your strengths and weaknesses. Our imperfections are what make us unique and beautiful. Instead of spending a lifetime trying to change yourself, work with what you have. Focus on the journey rather than the destination.

If you strive for perfection, you may miss out on opportunities. Whether it be a missed deadline or not being able to take on new customers, minimising profits due to a higher labour cost or not being satisfied with the outcome, perfection can have a negative effect on your work and personal life. If you get fixated on the notion of delivering the perfect product, report, or customer experience, consider the opportunity cost. How much extra time, resources, and possibly money are you investing in the outcome compared to if you got it to being good and leaving it at that?

To paraphrase Zig Zigler: you don't have to be good to start, you just have to start to be good. With time comes knowledge and experience. The world deserves to see what you are capable of, and if you hide behind the perfection veil, the world will miss out.

Ask yourself:

1. How do you define perfection?
2. Do you strive for perfection?
3. How does striving for perfection make you feel?
4. Why do you feel the urge to be perfect?
5. When has perfection hindered your progress?

Chapter 4

CHANGING YOUR PERSPECTIVE—FROM VICTIM TO SOLUTION-SEEKER

I am convinced that life is 10% what happens
to you and 90% how you respond to it.
—CHARLES R SWINDOLL

When I turned twenty-five, I had what I'd call a 'quarter-century crisis'. Suddenly, I felt a mix of emotions ranging from sadness to frustration. Sad because I have been alive for twenty-five years and I felt like I hadn't achieved much of anything, and frustrated because I didn't know what I wanted to spend my life doing. For a few weeks following my birthday, I wasn't in a good mood. I was completely immersed in feeling sorry and frustrated for myself. I thought I'd find the answer to my problems in books or asking others for their opinions but that didn't yield any answers. When I was actually able to hear what my partner had to say (which was, 'Why not try different things, make time for hobbies, and have some downtime?') I was able to start looking for a solution to my problem.

I started to look for creative workshops to discover new hobbies and I began to read books that helped me learn more about myself. Instead of asking for answers from others, I decided to look within and learn about the person I was and hoped to become. I could have stayed a victim and spent more time wallowing about not having done much with my life, but instead I chose to change my perspective and take action. I also reflected on my achievements and it helped me realise that I have done fun things like travel, live overseas, and complete a bachelor's degree.

There are variables beyond our control, so while we may not be in complete control of every situation that we find ourselves in, we do have control over how we respond. I like to use the metaphor of wearing glasses. You can view the world through a negative lens in which you believe that the world is against you, and so you play a victim of your circumstances by relinquishing your power.[6] Or you can view the world through a more positive lens and seek out solutions. When you're playing the victim, you often become focused on the past, wondering why it happened to you. You begin to operate with less energy. When you dwell on a situation and ask 'why me?', you won't be led to a solution. If you want to find a solution, change the question. Ask yourself 'why is this happening for me' and be open to the answers. See it as an opportunity to grow.

While it's true that our brains have a negativity bias, we have the ability to train our brains to focus on the positive.[7] Those who have a fixed mindset tend to ignore this possibility and see the world as they perceive it to be, but those with a growth mindset would be willing to try this. Think about people you have interacted with over the years: would you prefer to speak to an uplifting and joyous person or someone who just wants to complain? When reflecting on this question, use it as a guide as to how you respond to situations.

It may seem easier to play the victim, but try to take the high road and seek out solutions. I know there have been times when I've wondered why things always happen to me, such as when I was single and it felt like everyone else had a partner but me, and my situation remained unchanged. When you play the victim card, you are essentially agreeing with your situation and become stuck because you believe that you don't have the power to change your situation.

When I find myself upset with a situation which is not life-altering, I try to check in with myself and ask 'will this bother me in five years' time?' Most of the time, the answer is no, and from there, I try to let it go as soon as possible. It's not always easy, but I'd rather let it go than remain stuck where I am. If we spend our entire lives sweating the small stuff, playing the victim, and always wondering why things are happening *to* us rather than *for* us, we miss out on so much. We miss out on the opportunities that come from challenging situations, personal growth, and life lessons because we aren't willing to see past what happened. More than that—we miss the magic. When you're in a bad mood, it's hard to appreciate the present moment because you're not willing to see beyond the negatives.

John Gottman and Robert Levenson's work suggests that there is a ratio of 5:1 for positive and negative experiences.[8] That is, in order to counteract one negative, it takes five positives. As our brains have a negativity bias, the ratio of negative to positive is quite high. If we can train our minds to scan our environment for positives, we can limit the impact that negatives have on our moods. When we change our perspective, we shift our focus. Just as using keywords helps to you to yield a more specific result, so too can focusing on specific things each day to help you overcome the negative bias in your mind. It may feel strange at first, but with practice it will get easier.

Try setting an intention to look for the good throughout your day, whether that be appreciating the bright colours around you, nice aromas, a warm smile, or a song that makes you want to count the beat; the choice is yours.

To paraphrase Randy Pausch, we cannot control the deck of cards we are given but we have the power to choose how we react.[9] We can choose to see and focus on the negatives or we can search for a positive. Try not to take it personally; learn to detach from the situation and seek out what the situation is trying to teach you. Solutions will find you when you're not allowing the fear complex to overcome your mind. Become a solution seeker and you'll be able to see what you're truly capable of.

Chapter 5

CHANGE IS INEVITABLE

Change is good, even if it doesn't always seem like it at the time. It reminds us that life is finite, and if we learn to accept that change is an inevitable part of life, we can be more present, grateful, and loving. We can appreciate what we have, tell our loved ones what they mean to us, and have contingency plans in place for any what-if scenarios.

At the end of the day, we can either embrace change or resist it. Not all change is welcomed with open arms, but we can't control what happens, only how we respond. We are creatures of habit—some more than others, but we like stability. When change comes and it's unexpected, we all react differently. At the time of writing this book, we are currently living in an unprecedented time, thanks to COVID-19. Now, this one virus has had a global impact and it's unclear when lives will return to what we once considered normal. All the things we took for granted such as the ability to travel, spend time with loved ones, buy multiple items at the supermarket, and having a job were suddenly taken away. When restrictions were being introduced and then gradually became stricter, it was a lot of information to process. It is in times like these that we can either fight the change or embrace that this is now our situation and work with it as best we can. You can either adapt or fight when major changes happen. You can choose how you invest your time and energy.

Change at work may impact you more than a road closure which forces you to change the way you drive home. It's about the size, type, nature, and how much control you have over the change. When change feels like you have been blindsided, it may take you longer to process and welcome the change. It is important to remember that you do not always need to like the change that is happening, but you should try to accept it. Acceptance is the only way to move forward. When you spend all your energy resisting the change, it limits your ability to move on.

We can take time to reflect on how things were, but we must learn to accept it can never revert back to the way it was, no matter how much we would like it to. Each of us has our own set of change absorbers which allows us to accept change up until a certain point. Some changes are welcomed with open arms, such as moving on to a new job, moving out of home, or falling in love. Then there are other changes which bring us to a standstill, such as getting fired, the loss of a loved one, or a relationship fallout. We all have to handle positive and negative changes in our lives—unfortunately, we can't pick one and not the other. Changes that happen unexpectedly often take longer to accept. When we get blindsided by change, we become reactive, but when we anticipate the change, we can be proactive. The less control we have over the change, the more we may try to resist it.

Change provides us with an opportunity to grow. Sometimes it hurts our ego, breaks our heart and makes our souls feel heavy, but those feelings will ease with time. It is normal to mourn and feel something, but it is important to move through and past these feelings rather than dwelling on them. When you fight the change, you're attempting to change a moment that has already happened. We can only change our present and future, not the past. Fighting or resisting it is a waste of precious time and energy you won't get back. When you remain stuck, you cannot move forward, and it is impossible to move backwards. During these times, remember that without change, there can be no growth, no movement, and no progression. It is an inevitable part of life. We may not be able to control the changes we may experience during our lifetime, but we can alter how we handle each change.

Big changes, such as moving out of home, moving house, finishing school, changing jobs, starting a family, beginning or ending a relationship, or buying a car can impact many parts of our life. Some changes impact one area while others can impact more.

With big impact changes, it's important to acknowledge the change, check in to how you are feeling, and nurture yourself through the change process. Allow yourself to be present, acknowledge how you are feeling and that the transitional phase is temporary. You have experienced change before and will again.

Ask yourself:

1. What change do you handle with grace?
2. What change do you struggle to deal with?
3. Are you pro-change or anti-change?
4. Do you perceive change as a positive or negative?

Chapter 6

POSITIVE SELF-TALK

What you think, you become.
—BUDDHA.

The perfect person doesn't exist. If we aim for perfection, we lose ourselves along the way because we are trying to please others. You cannot be everything to everyone. It's okay to love yourself exactly as you are—flaws and all. We can only aim to be the best version of ourselves and accept our imperfections. When we make a mistake or go through a challenging time, be kind rather than blame yourself. Just because something went wrong, that doesn't mean you're incompetent, a failure, or unintelligent. It simply means you are human. Rather than belittle yourself, learn from the challenges and see it as an opportunity to grow. You are not a failure if you fail; it is merely a moment in time which doesn't define who you are.

From a young age, we are usually taught to treat others with kindness as well as to treat them how we would like to be treated in return. Yet when it comes to ourselves, our internal dialogue and perspective of ourselves doesn't reflect this. We are hard on ourselves, and yet, if we were talking to a loved one about the same situation, our words would be completely different. Each of us has our own insecurities and things we'd change about ourselves, but why? Is the desire for change coming from a place of love or fear? Necessity or want? When you take fear-based action such as becoming obsessed with what you're eating in order to maintain the ideal figure, it isn't healthy. You're associating your value and worthiness to be loved by others with a number on the scale. Even if you reach that number, you likely won't feel satisfied. The void is still there and it's because you aren't happy within yourself.

I've been there. I used to restrict my calories and over exercise in order to stay slim. Even when I got down to an Australian size 4–6, I still wasn't happy. I'd always talk down to myself and see myself as looking fat or ugly. I wanted to lose more weight. Then, unexpectedly I gained about four kilograms in one month and I couldn't work out why. Soon after, it was ten kilograms in total that I gained. Even a year later, as I'm writing this, I'm still carrying the extra weight, and yet I'm feeling okay within myself. I've changed the way I look at myself. I'm trying to speak to myself with love and acknowledge the steps I'm taking to be healthier rather than being afraid that people won't love me because I've put on some weight. Happiness is an inside job; it cannot come from external things as there will always be a void or fear of losing it.

If you want to change the way you perceive yourself, begin by changing how you speak to yourself. For many of us, our internal dialogue is cruel. We don't treat ourselves with love and respect. It's like we are bullying ourselves. While there's no one reason we speak to ourselves in this way, it could be because we are not able to accept the person we are. We seem to be acutely aware of our flaws and so we remind ourselves about them. An example of this is when we look in the mirror and see a perceived version of ourselves. If we believe we have bad skin or a flabby stomach, this will be what we focus on. What seems like a huge flaw is typically not noticed by others. Of course, we each have blind spots— the parts of ourselves we don't see. Dwelling on the negative won't make it any better. Say, for instance, that you're having a good hair day: would you acknowledge this? Or would you find something else to focus on instead, like how you think your thighs look big that day? Our negative self-talk is a waste of energy and hurts our self-confidence.

We are only human. We each have our own strengths and weaknesses and we have the choice to decide whether we want to spend our lives being in constant disagreement with ourselves, trying to change the way we look to match some perceived perfection we are striving towards, or we can choose to love ourselves as we are. Self-acceptance and belief looks good on every person. If you feel good, accept it, and when you get a compliment, say 'thank you' rather than deflecting.

Be kind to yourself. Too often, we hold ourselves to a high standard and kick ourselves when we fall short. Rather than celebrating our journey so far, we hold ourselves accountable for a mess-up. We hopefully wouldn't speak to loved ones in this manner, so why do we do it with ourselves? Love starts with you. Learn to love yourself unconditionally, and if there are things you want to change, take action and be kind to yourself in the process. If you're trying to build muscle, acknowledge the steps you're taking rather than telling yourself that you're weak and will never be strong. That kind of self-talk will get you nowhere if you focus on the latter. We need to accept ourselves for who we are and who we are becoming and celebrate the good and bad. We are human. We are not striving for perfection, just to be better than the person we were yesterday. Own your victories and learn from challenges. That's how you grow and evolve.

When you say something negative to yourself, flip it. Make it positive. If you like quotes and mantras, create one that resonates with you and say it daily.

Ask yourself:

1. List five things you love about yourself.
2. On a scale of 1 to 10, how do you feel about yourself?
3. What do you want to change about yourself?
4. Why do you feel the need to change yourself?
5. What is a positive affirmation you can say to yourself when negative thoughts come creeping in?
6. When do you put yourself down?
7. Write down a negative thing you say to yourself. Next to it, write down a positive.

Chapter 7

COMPARISON AND SOCIAL MEDIA

Never compare your beginning to someone else's middle.
—JON ACUFF

Too often, we compare what we have or haven't achieved to others. When we are comparing our lives to others, we get tunnel vision. We forget that each of us has our own story. We only see the effort that we are personally putting in. We don't know the sacrifices, challenges, and time that others have invested into their goals. So, when we compare, it isn't a like-for-like comparison. We are essentially comparing our whole life to the fragments we see of another's.

It's easy to get caught up in the 'I'm not enough' mindset or continuously comparing your life to those around you, whether on a digital platform or in real life. Many of us have access to social media and technology 24/7 which constantly floods our feeds with people who seem to have it all. As a result, comparison can be never-ending. How often do you put down your phone after scrolling through social media feeds feeling good? How many times do you feel guilty, anxious, stressed, or jealous? If you mainly feel negative emotions afterwards you may want to reflect on why you feel that way, as well as the pages/people/ businesses that are making you feel negatively. Try to use social media in a way that inspires you rather than drains your energy. If it doesn't serve you well, then leave it be.

Think of the time spent comparing yourself to others in terms of the return on investment. What are you getting in return for the time and energy you invest into this? Chances are it's a whole lot of negative emotions, dissatisfaction, and a lack of motivation. If you're continuously focusing on what others are doing, you forget to run your own race. Don't be a spectator in your own life.

We strive for what we feel we should be, and even when we are achieving our own goals, we look at what others are doing (including celebrities, brand ambassadors, friends, and so forth) and we make ourselves feel small. Comparison is the thief of happiness. It often leads to negative feelings rather than helping you get results. Instead of looking at what you are doing compared to others, focus on yourself. If you want to compare, compare who you were to who you are now. Use comparison as a reflective tool to look at the progress you have made. Make it empowering rather than belittling.

Focusing on the success of others is not beneficial if you're using it as a way to avoid working toward your goals. If you're comparing your life to others and constantly telling yourself what they have isn't possible for you, then of course it won't be! This is if you're comparing yourself to someone who has something that you are striving for. Whether it be quitting your nine-to-five to become a freelancer, being self-employed, working from home, buying a house, getting married, having a successful blog or influencer status—the list is endless. What they have, you can have too if you apply your skills and knowledge and work for it. There is enough to go around. Apply the abundance mindset and trust that there is enough to go around rather than making excuses. You have to put in the effort to get to where you want to be. It's not as easy as wishing it into happening. The more time you spend comparing yourself to others, the less time you have to work on your goals and succeed. Where your time goes, your energy flows. So why not do a habit switch and swap the comparing for achieving?

Over the past few years, I have tried hard to limit how much I compare myself to others. I removed accounts from my social media feeds that made me feel lousy and I've invested more time and energy into working on projects that fill me with joy. I still have my moments when I compare myself to others, and now I'm aware of how it makes me feel, I try not to let myself get caught up in it. The same goes for comparing myself to who I was, especially when it comes to my appearance. I gained some weight suddenly, and more than a year and a half later, I haven't been able to move it all. I look back at old photos of my 'skinny' self and I feel sad. Then I go online and see that others also feel this way and that it's normal to feel sad sometimes. Comparison with just yourself can also have a negative effect on you depending on what you're comparing. The key takeaway is to notice how you feel after you've compared yourself to someone else or your former self. If it's negative, try to call yourself out on it, and if it's positive, acknowledge the good feelings.

The success of others is of no consequence to yours. Comparison can be beneficial when it fuels you rather than drains you. If you can compare yourself to others in a positive way to motivate you and learn from others rather than making you feel envious and so forth, then you feel better for it. Create your own path by being yourself rather than living in the shadows of another.

For a short while, I removed Instagram and Facebook from my phone. I also deleted my Instagram account and started again because I was following accounts that were not boosting my self-esteem. I didn't like the feeling I would get from interacting with the platform, so I made a conscious decision to change it.

I saw the luxurious lives that influencers, models, and other high-profile people on Instagram seem to lead. I accepted this as the complete truth and thought *How do they get to wear all of these amazing clothes, attend events, and look some glamorous all the time?* I didn't take the time to stop and question what I saw. Was the post sponsored? Do they have staff who arrange their meals and schedules, or do they outsource general things such as cleaning a house or doing their laundry? We look at others and are amazed at the lifestyle they have or how full their lives seem to be, travelling from one place to the next yet we just see their public façade and nothing more. That's not to say that some people have built incredible lives for themselves, but when you compare yourself to them and think what they have is unattainable, it can have a negative impact on your mood and self-esteem.

With all this being said, is it time for you to do an audit on your social media accounts? Are you following accounts that make you feel good and give you a boost of happiness or do you find yourself falling down the rabbit hole and getting into a bad mood? Create a feed that inspires you to grow rather than files you with envy, sadness, or a lack of confidence as a result of comparison.

Once you become aware of how you feel, you can decide if the feelings are aligned with how you want to feel or if a change is needed.

Ask yourself:

1. What social media platforms do I use and why?
2. How much time do I spend on social media each day?
3. How do I feel after scrolling through a social media feed?
4. What time/s of the day do I scroll through social media?
5. Who do I follow on social media and why?

Chapter 8

OVERCOMING DOUBTS

Have you ever felt like you were out of your depth? Like you were the only person who didn't know what they were doing? You may have experienced this feeling when you started a new job, moved somewhere new, or had a major change in your life. It's a fear-based feeling of doubt which leads you to believe that you are not worthy or capable of something. This feeling usually presents itself in situations where you are starting something new, and even though you may have the skills required, you feel like you are just pretending that you know how to do or be something.

Doubt often surfaces when you are stepping out of your comfort zone. Personally, it has surfaced in new relationships as a result of feeling like I am not worthy or deserving of being loved by someone else. Even though I am happily engaged to my fiancé, I still have doubts. I still feel like he'll wake up one day and wonder why he's with me. As he has kindly assured me many times before, it won't happen, but it still doesn't stop the doubt from coming back in. More broadly, these feelings surface when I feel vulnerable or lack self-belief.

Doubt surfaces in different ways for each of us. To begin to overcome your feelings of doubt, you'll need to know when it surfaces for you.

If you lack confidence, it may be time to turn inward and reflect on who you are and what makes you amazing. Once you begin to learn to love yourself for all that you are, you can separate yourself from such thoughts when they enter your mind. You can accept that you may not know all the answers, but with time, you will learn and be better. Acknowledge the thoughts and remind yourself that you are safe.

If doubt appears when you are doing something new, whether it's a new job or trying a new recipe or activity, stop and take a deep breath. Focus on the moment and remind yourself that you are capable of stepping out of your comfort zone and excelling. In the words of Robin Sharma, 'Every master was once a beginner. Every pro was once an amateur.'

We don't need to buy into these thoughts; it's not the truth. I like to think of doubt as having many personas. If you overcome the initial self-doubt and begin something new, it tries to convince you that you're a fraud and don't know what you're doing. Of course it's true! You're doing something you haven't done before—it's unchartered territory.

So, when doubt appears, we have two options: let it control how we handle a situation or to acknowledge the feeling and challenge it. When we get curious about our doubts and challenge our thoughts, we can establish whether it's a false 'truth' we are telling ourselves. Even when we don't feel up to the challenge, all we can do is try to do our best and see what eventuates.

Regardless of who you are, we all have experienced this feeling before. Just as you are acutely aware of a flaw, you may feel like you are inadequate at times. The cause of the feeling may be due to doubt, fear, or a limited self-belief. Be kind to yourself when you are venturing out of your comfort zone and know that you will come to fill the knowledge gaps.

Chapter 9

WHAT MAKES YOU FEEL GOOD?

Because emotions are subjective, we each have our own definition of what feeling good feels like and looks like. What makes me feel good may make you feel terrible and vice versa. If you're not sure what makes you feel good, it's time for a little introspection.

Give yourself permission to fill your days with moments, activities, and experiences that light you up and, in turn, make you feel good. You deserve to feel good every day.

Instead of waiting for future happiness or associating happiness with external factors, such as 'I'll be happier when I lose ten kilograms' or 'I'll be happy when I have a higher-paying job', start today. Fill your days with things that make you feel good. When you're feeling good, you can experience positive emotions such as joy, happiness, and contentment.

Build a solid foundation, starting with yourself. If you cannot be happy within yourself, then you may never be able to fill the void with external things. By working out what makes you feel good, you can find ways of incorporating these activities into each day. While not every day can be our ideal day, we can still allocate time to do something which makes us feel good. Joy is a powerful emotion which can be found in any moment if we allow ourselves to feel it.

How can you start to transform your days from being mediocre to wonderful? What activities, people, or environments light you up? When we surround ourselves with people who drain our energy, in environments that leave us feeling empty, or participate in life in a passive way, then we become bored and indifferent.

While it may not be possible to do everything you want each day of your life, you can find ways to enhance your life. Rather than waiting until a weekend, holiday, or break to celebrate life, find ways to enhance each day. Whether it be taking ten minutes to read, going for a walk, playing a video game, learning something new, writing or reading a blog post, dancing to music, speaking to a loved one, or eating a home cooked meal, the more frequently we fill our days with something which makes us feel good, the better we begin to feel.

If you work in an office, can you decorate your work area to make you want to work there? It may be something simple like a new desktop wallpaper, a pen which makes you want to write, a photo of someone or something that you love, or a sentimental item that brings you joy. Alternatively, why not wear outfits (if you're not allocated a uniform) that represents you? If you like bold colours, why not wear something colourful which makes you feel good?

When we find ways to brighten up our days, we feel better. Once our lower-order needs (according to Maslow's Hierarchy of Needs[10]) such as food, shelter, safety, and loved ones are met, we can begin to look for other ways to fulfil our sense of purpose and satisfaction, whether it be job satisfaction, embarking on a spiritual quest, or trying to find and then fulfil our purpose in life.

Ask yourself:

1. What activities make you feel good?
2. Do you allocate time daily to do something that makes you feel good?
3. Allocate time each day for thirty days to do something that makes you feel good and monitor how you feel. Do you feel happier or more energised?

Chapter 10

WHAT'S YOUR LEGACY?

Legacy, in the context of this book, relates to the story of your life. It's about the experiences you had, the goals you accomplished, the challenges you overcame, the relationships you formed, the places you travelled, and much more. It is what you leave behind—the tangible and intangible—and it is what you are remembered by others for. What do you want to be remembered as?

Trying to think of what you want to achieve in your lifetime can be overwhelming. Our goals change, and what we thought we once wanted may not always be the same. Instead, take a moment to reflect on what you would like your legacy to be. What do you want to leave behind? If you think of the mark you want to make on the world and the kind of life you hope to lead, it can assist you in working out what you can do in the present.

While having a legacy doesn't guarantee that it will be exactly how others perceive you and remember you, it does give you a blueprint in terms of how to conduct yourself. If you value travel, do you want to be remembered as adventurous or as a couch potato? Your actions will shape your legacy.

Just as setting short term and long term goals is important to keep you focused and progressing towards a bigger-picture goal, determining your legacy can help you establish where you are and where you want to be. Your legacy relates to your life as a whole, including the person you are, the way you make others feel, the roles you had, the way you contributed to the community, and the relationships you nurtured.

If you feel stuck, unsure of who you are and what you want from life, this exercise can give you some guidance.

Ask yourself:

1. What are my greatest accomplishments?
2. What mark do I want to leave on the world?
3. If today is my last day, what would others say about me?

Am I living a fulfilling life?

If you have people around you who you are happy to discuss this topic with, ask them to provide you with insight about how they see you, what you bring to their life, and why they're grateful to have you in their life. By seeking comments from others, you are able to determine what changes you may need to make to live a more meaningful life.

Many of us hope that we are able to leave the world in a better state than when we entered into it so the generations that come after us are cared for. By understanding what you want your legacy to be, you can change your behaviours, actions, and goals to work towards creating it. Determine the mark you want to make and work on making it happen.

Everyone's legacy is different. Some may be remembered as unique, fun, and creative while others may be remembered as a family person: kind and loving. Whatever your legacy is, treasure it and live a life that will fulfil it.

Chapter 11

LEARNING TO SAY 'NO'.

If you're not saying 'HELL YEAH!' about something, say 'no'.
—DEREK SIVERS

'No' is a small word, and yet it is hard to say. Many of us are people-pleasers and we fear what saying no means. We fear that if we say no to others, we will be perceived as not being helpful, being selfish, ungrateful, or not a team player. The truth is, we get to choose what we say yes to and how we spend our finite time on Earth. There is only so much you can do each day so be careful of what you say yes to.

Whether we say yes or no, there's a price to pay. The price is time lost. It's the time that could have been spent with loved ones, working on a passion project, or relaxing. We have all had times where we have said yes when we wished we had said no and vice versa. Our time is finite and it's your choice how you spend your time. Take time to consider the opportunity cost. According to the *Concise Encyclopedia of Economics,* 'opportunity cost' is a term used by economists to determine the value of the next-highest-valued alternative use of a resource. In the context of this chapter, the resource is time. For instance, if I choose to go out for dinner rather than stay in and cook, I am forgoing money and time that I could have spent at home.

What are you giving up in order to do something? We tend to say yes without thinking about what we're giving up and this is risky because the yeses add up overtime. Compound yeses limit your ability to focus on the tasks that will get you towards your goal. If you genuinely know it is not an event or opportunity you want to accept, say no. We cannot please everyone, and if we spend our lives saying yes to be polite, we will not have time to focus on our goals or ambitions.

If saying yes to something right now causes you stress, you can either say no or 'not right now'. Don't feel guilty for saying no. We get to choose how we spend our time, and if there is something else of greater value or priority to you, invest your time there.

Regardless of who we are, we all have something in common—the number of hours we have in a day. What separates successful people from those who are stuck where they are is their mindset and how they allocate their time. Words without action are simply words. If you want to get something done, you need to start. If you set an intention for the day to achieve certain things, protect your time, and if you need to say no, then do so. We simply cannot do everything in a day.

Learning to say no isn't easy. It takes practice. If you are someone who struggles to say no to others without feeling guilty, you may want to create healthy boundaries which will empower you to say no to things that don't make you feel good.

Before you can say no, it's important to know what matters to you. To begin, write down your top five values and your top three priorities. If it helps, you can make a separate list for work and your personal life.

Next, write down a list of your current and upcoming commitments. Rank your commitments on a scale from 1 to 10 with 1 being 'I'm dreading it' to 10 'it lights me up.' Once you've completed this exercise, take a moment to see where your commitments are all ranked. Are most of your commitments on the lower or upper end of the scale? This is your starting point. From here you can begin to protect your time by creating healthy boundaries and slowly starting to fill your days with commitments that light you up rather than fill you with dread.

Once you've established what your priorities are, it makes it easier to say no to things that aren't contributing to what you want to achieve. You can start to say no or not right now to things that reduce your time to focus on hobbies, exercise, projects, or anything else that lights you up. Loved ones will still love you if you say no. Business opportunities will still exist if you say no.

Saying no to family events is something I struggle with. I value family and enjoy spending time with loved ones but there are some days when I'd rather spend my time working on a project (such as this book) or go for a walk. A few years ago, I went to a pool party to celebrate the birthday of my partner's brother. I'm not someone who enjoys swimming or large crowds of unfamiliar faces. I said yes to be polite, but I would've preferred to have said no. I didn't have the best time because I didn't want to be there. So now when the annual pool party happens, I politely say no. I'd rather go to an event and be happy than dread going. It also means I get to spend that time on something I value more.

We try to avoid cancelling appointments and plans with others, but we are comfortable cancelling the appointments we make with ourselves. It is not selfish to put yourself first and make your goals a priority. When you are thriving, you put out a positive energy into the world. When it's time for the safety briefing on aeroplanes, we are instructed by the cabin crew to fit our own oxygen mask first before helping others.

Saying no to what doesn't feel right, doesn't interest you, or isn't a priority for you allows you to put yourself first. Learn to value your time and think of it as a finite resource. Any time you give away is gone. If you are struggling, frustrated, and burnt out, you're not going to perform at your best. To be able to give more to others, you need to start protecting your time, focus on your goals, and limit distractions. If the trade-off for saying yes to something is not worth it, then say no. If you've been a yes person, learning to say no without feeling guilt can be challenging. Begin by saying no to one thing and acknowledge how you feel. A no doesn't need to be permanent—it may simply mean 'not now'.

Honour yourself including your dreams, goals, and plans. Listen to your inner voice, if you instinctively say a silent no to yourself and you know it isn't essential that you attend then don't feel obligated to say yes. Let the inviter down with a constructive no and keep it simple. You don't need to make up a lavish excuse as to why you can't go— just keep it simple. Nos don't need a justification. People will appreciate your honesty if you just say no upfront rather than say yes and cancel last-minute.

In my late teens and early twenties, I was great at saying yes and changing my mind later. When the day arrived, I was filled with anxiety because I knew I didn't want to go. So, I would cancel last-minute with a flimsy excuse. I discovered that once you begin to fall into the habit of saying yes then no, people begin to perceive you as being flaky. So, you either don't get included in outings or people don't expect you to come. It wasn't really until I began having people cancel plans on me at the last minute that I realised how frustrating it was. I didn't really take time to consider the consequences of my actions and how it impacted others until I was on the receiving end. I had a realisation after I returned home from Canada and decided that I needed (and wanted) to act with more integrity. This meant saying no when needed and sticking to my yeses when I agreed to go somewhere or do something. I don't always get it right, but I have definitely moved on from my flaky days.

There have been many times in my life when I have agreed to do something, go somewhere, or spend time with a person or people whom I'd rather not and it's been a source of stress leading up the event. Saying yes when I wanted to say no has caused me to cancel last-minute, act like a child by getting upset at others, or to drag my feet in an attempt to get someone else to give me permission to not attend. There have been times when I have upheld my yes and it's been a pleasant experience, but I know I would have preferred to have been doing something else or being somewhere else.

Yes may be an instant response when you're put on the spot. If being put on the spot results in you saying yes without thought, take a moment to pause. Give yourself time to consider your decision rather than saying yes automatically and wanting to backtrack later. If you're not wanting to provide an answer straight away, advise the person that you will get back to them in due time. You may say you'll give them an answer in a few hours, by the end of the day, or end of the week, but it gives you a chance to consider your answer. Regardless of your answer, you have taken time to consider the opportunity cost and generally people will appreciate that you have taken time to think about your response.

With that being said, if you're indifferent to saying yes and it won't impact your schedule a great deal if you do attend, you could say yes if it means a lot to the other person.

The objective with learning to say no is to take control back. Your time is precious; once a moment has passed it cannot be undone, so you want to ensure that you are spending your moments how you want to. Whether you say yes or no, ensure it is a conscious choice you have made rather than allowing others to determine how you spend your time. It may not seem like a major problem to give your power away to others by saying yes to please them, but it's at your own cost. At first you may feel guilty for saying no. It feels selfish to put yourself first, but it isn't. Your time is a precious resource, and if you fill your days with things that don't light you up, you're not going to have a happy life. If others are used to hearing you say yes, they may be taken aback when you start saying no. Don't let this rattle you.

We have the ability to shape our future, and each yes or no means a possible future reality will or won't happen as a result. If you want to start creating a life that excites you, you need to start valuing your time. Decide how you want to fill your days; get selective. If you say yes when you mean no, you're contradicting yourself. It's much easier to say no upfront than it is to cancel last-minute with a flimsy excuse. You save energy and time by being honest with yourself and others.

It's okay to say no. We weren't created to be people-pleasers, and sometimes a no is needed. If you say yes to every invitation, you may end up spreading yourself too thin, getting stressed out, and feeling overworked and underappreciated. Saying no allows you to focus more on the things that matter to you. Save your yeses for events which inspire you, support others, and don't take away from your goals. Take time to consider your answer if needed; you don't always need to give your answer straight away. Find your status quo and respect yourself enough to give an honest answer.

Ask yourself:

Before saying yes or no, consider the following:

1. What am I giving up?
2. What is the opportunity cost?
3. Who do you find it hard to say no to?
4. If you are a yes person, how can you find ways to give yourself time to think of your response?
5. How do you react when it's time to do something you wish you had said no to doing?

Chapter 12

WHAT ARE YOU HOLDING ONTO?

As children, we live life fearlessly. We haven't developed filters or lenses through which we view the world. So instead, we see the world through wide eyes, our imaginations run wild, and we aren't afraid to say the truth because we don't know otherwise. As the years progress, our thoughts and actions are shaped by many things such as culture, ideologies, beliefs, values, education, and experiences. Social conditioning takes place, and we start to create our own set of lenses through which we view the world. It is during this time that we begin to hold on to emotional baggage.

Some baggage may only stay with you momentarily but other baggage can be carried around for a lifetime. We collect emotional baggage consciously or subconsciously and carry it around with us wherever we go. Rarely do we do an audit of what we are traipsing around with, and over the years the baggage can weigh us down. It impacts our decisions and how we perceive ourselves and others. Depending on the baggage, it can also have health consequences.

As the years go by, we accumulate more emotional baggage. We have two options: to continue to carry this excess baggage or find ways to let it go. When we are unable to move due to the baggage we are carrying, we become stuck where we are. Fear takes over and we limit ourselves based on past experiences. For example, if you were bullied by others at school, you may find it hard to make friends or trust others. If you have been in toxic relationships, you may have intimacy and trust issues. While the emotional responses are real and valid, it may be time to consider whether this baggage is weighing you down and preventing you from living the life you're capable of. With that being said, if you are holding onto something and you're not sure how to let go of it, please consider seeking advice from a professional.

Before the baggage gets to be too much to handle, try to consider what you are holding onto, how long it has been with you, and if you need it anymore. If it no longer serves you, try to find a way to leave it behind. Just as clutter takes up unneeded space in our homes, so does emotional baggage. It weighs you down and you create false truths based on the baggage. You begin to make assumptions, feel insecure, or act out of fear rather than love.

If you are able to do a baggage audit and let some go, you will begin to feel free again. Some people seem to carry chips on their shoulders for decades, sometimes even to their grave. These suitcases can limit their growth.

The more baggage we carry, the harder it is to keep moving forward.

As these suitcases are intangible, others cannot see what you are carrying around and vice versa. Some days, the weight of the world seems to be balanced on your shoulders, and on days such as those, ask yourself what is one thing you can remove from your suitcase? The same applies for days when you are tempted to add something new to your suitcase. Take time to ask whether it is worthwhile packing it.

Challenge your beliefs and the reasons why you are still carrying around your baggage, because often it is based on a false truth or another's perception of you. Once you begin to define who you are and what your values are and have a strong sense of self and self-belief, you can make more rational decisions about what you carry with you.

Ask yourself:

1. What baggage are you carrying around with you?
2. How long have you been holding onto it?
3. Why are you holding onto this baggage?
4. What baggage are you prepared to let go of?

Chapter 13

LEAVING THE PAST IN THE PAST

You can either allow your past to control your present and future or you can let it go. We cannot rewrite the past, but we can create a new present and future if we choose to. Most of the time, we either live in the past or dream about the future. Our thoughts can rule our minds, and unless we are able to reflect on our habits, personality traits, and triggers, we will be on a continuous loop.

In his book *Breaking the Habit of Being Yourself*, Joe Dispenza explains how we can get caught in a loop where our personality reflects our personal reality.[11] The way in which we act can affect the way we perceive the world, our situation, and the opportunities we do and don't take. In order to change, we must break the habit of being ourselves by considering what our unconscious behaviours are and deciding whether they are worth our energy in the future. Not all of our habits and behaviours serve us well. Instead of passively experiencing cause and effect, we can choose to be the ones *causing* an effect. Rather than allowing your past to determine your future, you can let go of what no longer serves you. By releasing that which no longer serves you, you can make space for new things moving forward.

There are times when we focus on variables that we cannot control rather than those we can. We place a great emphasis on trying to control the outcome, and when the result is different, we aren't content. Over time, we get accustomed to playing the victim card rather than holding ourselves accountable. If you're wanting to become the best version of yourself, then you will need to be accountable for your actions and decisions. While it is easy to pass the blame to others or play the victim, it takes courage to hold yourself accountable. But just like any skill, practice makes it easier over time.

There is a quote we hear time and again—often misattributed to Einstein—that says, 'Insanity is doing the same thing over and over again, but expecting different results.' It is true the same actions will yield the same results. If you want a different result, change your approach. Learn from your experiences—the good and bad—and trust that you did the best you could with what you had.

Hindsight can be a hindrance to progress because we look back at a situation and think of what we would have done differently. The only thing is, we have more knowledge in the present than we did back then so it's not an equal comparison. Instead, look for the lesson and move forward rather than spending time thinking of what you would do differently if history repeated itself.

Not all moments are meant to last, which is what makes them special. Sometimes, we hold on too tightly to what is not meant for us because we fear that if we let it go, we won't get it back—that the universe gave us one chance and that's it. Consider this: if you didn't let go of a relationship that wasn't right for you, then you wouldn't free yourself up to allow a greater love to find you. Release your grip, have faith, and trust that when you surrender, what is meant for you will find its way to you.

Holding on to something and trying to make it work when it doesn't is not the best use of your time and energy. You end up spending mental energy trying to convince yourself that you are happy, content, satisfied, and so forth, when you know in your heart it isn't right. Let it go; look forwards rather than back. When we are living in the past or leading a life not meant for us, we often miss what has been staring us in the face all along and block ourselves from new opportunities.

Life doesn't stand still while you the relive the past. Be brave enough to welcome newness into your life. Learn from the past, but don't let it define and limit you.

EMOTIONALLY OR ENERGETICALLY DRAINED— WHAT DOES IT MEAN?

Life has its seasons, and there are times when we feel emotionally drained as a result of a stressful, traumatic, or testing time. If you have experienced the feeling of being emotionally drained, you can appreciate how challenging it is to recover. The feeling of exhaustion is linked to our energy levels. If you're continuously busy and don't give yourself time to stop and recover, you will burn out.

If you are in a constant state of emotional exhaustion or feeling drained, I would encourage you to try to find the root cause of this feeling. When we are in a continuous state of exhaustion, we are not doing ourselves any favours. We are unable to perform at our best, even when we have the best of intentions to do so. Simple tasks seem harder, such as getting out of bed in the morning or not dreading going to work. You become a shadow of your true self and it can have negative effects on your life, impacting relationships, your career, health, and wellbeing.

Let's think about a rechargeable battery for a moment: the greater the charge, the longer the battery is operational. When you start a day, your battery is at its fullest capacity after a nights' sleep. The previous day will have an impact on how well-charged your battery is in the morning. If you had a draining day, your charge may be lower as a result. If you're not recharging enough, then you will start the day with a lower threshold. You have a finite amount of energy and if you keep running on low power, you'll find it hard to function at your desired level because your energy levels aren't high enough.

During the day, our interactions with others can either add or subtract from our emotional levels. By the end of the day, you will have a limited amount of energy left. If you're in a constant state of exhaustion, it becomes increasingly difficult to recharge. You may start the day with a 10% charge. Easy tasks such as getting out of bed or being excited for another day become harder with anxiety and stress ruling your mind. When you get into this state of being, it's critical to do an audit and find out what is draining your emotional reservoir and find a way to resolve it. If you're wanting to replenish a low-to-empty amount of energy, it will take you longer to recharge than it would if you were topping up your high level again.

If you know you're going to require more energy, consciously make time to recharge rather than push through. If you run on empty for an extended period of time, you will become emotionally and energetically drained. You have two choices: recharge and monitor your energy levels, or keep pushing yourself until you reach the limit and point of exhaustion. While sometimes running near empty may be required for a short-term situation, it isn't a good habit to create.

As someone who has experienced this feeling, it had negative impacts on my relationships and motivation levels. I felt as though I was going through the motions, and while I was physically in a room, mentally I had checked out. If you recognise this feeling in yourself, try not to supress it as it can get worse if left unresolved.

Seek help—whether that be by confiding in a loved one or seeking professional help to assist you with finding ways to resolve this. Short-term, you can find ways each day to be more mindful, whether that be clearing your mind by exercising, focusing on your breath for a few moments, writing down a few items you're grateful for, or actively scanning the environment for things which fill you with a sense of joy.

Long-term, you will want to find the cause and find a way to resolve it. For instance, if it is your job that is draining you emotionally, you may not be able to hand in your resignation immediately; however, you can begin to search for a job which will be a better fit for you. Alternatively, if you like being part of the organisation, just not the role, you could have discussions with management to see if there is a role which you would be more suited to. Take time on your days off to recharge, and before/after work, try to do one thing which makes you feel good. If it's a relationship that is depleting you, have a conversation with the person, or if that isn't an option, put some space between you. Give yourself time to heal so you can drink from a full cup again.

Chapter 15

CHOOSING HAPPINESS

For me, happiness is the joy we feel striving after our potential.
—SHAWN ACHOR

The pursuit of happiness is a seemingly impossible journey. If you spend your life chasing it, you may not notice when it has arrived. Happiness means something different to each person. What makes me happy may bore you to tears. I like my bubble baths, hot cups of tea, going for nature walks, spending time with loved ones, and travelling. While these are a few of the things that make me happy, your list may look completely different and that is okay.

All I ask is: what do you associate with the word happiness? Many tie happiness to external factors and to the future. For instance, we might tell ourselves, 'In the future I'll be happy,' or 'When I have a higher paying job, I'll be happy'. If you're chasing future happiness, you miss out on the present. What is preventing you from being happy right now?

We can find happiness through the joy we feel in a moment. We can feel happy when we are in awe, feeling grateful, or appreciate what we have. When you see all that you have rather than what you perceive to be lacking, you can find peace. Happiness doesn't need to be conditional; you can simply choose to allow yourself to feel it.

There are times when we can choose happiness or a lower energy emotion. If you want to feel happier, you can choose to. You can shift how you feel. Go through the emotions and choose to feel better rather than sitting in a negative emotion. It is a way of experiencing the world and choosing what energy you bring to each day. It is about how you show up, how you treat others, and whether you look for the positive or a negative in the situation. Happiness is a higher energy emotion compared to fear, pessimism, or doubt. When you choose happiness, you experience joy and feel content and at peace with yourself.

When you are unhappy, you may seek momentary pleasure and, depending on the pleasure being sought, you may experience negative feelings that outweigh the moment. If you want to be happy, then you will need to define what happiness means to you.

What does happiness feel/taste/sound/smell/look like to you? You can create a wider definition of happiness if you incorporate all of your senses. Happiness may look like seeing your dog after a day at work or watching a sunset. It may sound like the voice of a loved one or hearing waves crash along the shore. It may taste like a hot drink or your favourite home-cooked meal. It may feel like a warm hug from a loved one, dancing in the rain, or seeing snow for the first time. Write down what happiness means to you without judgement and see what comes to mind.

If you believe that happiness is having a luxurious house decorated with high-quality furniture and walls with art and a garage filled with luxury vehicles then, by all means, pursue that. But if you feel true happiness when you feel connected to others, then why not find ways to add more of that into your life?

Another way to create happiness is to train your mind to see the good rather than focusing on the negative in each situation. You may want to start the day with a mantra, a kind word to yourself, and finding one thing to be grateful for. It could be something as simple as feeling rested after a deep slumber or being able to sleep next to a loved one. When you practice gratitude, you are able to celebrate the good and remind yourself of what you have in your life.

By focusing on the good in your life, you can become more present. You can appreciate what is in front of you rather than looking into the future. Celebrate what you have right now. Happiness is a magical feeling, so when you allow yourself to feel it, feel it deeply and for as long as you can. When fear tries to creep in to remind you that the feeling is too good to be true, acknowledge the thoughts and let them go. Give yourself the chance to be happy and when you can, choose happiness.

Chapter 16

OUTER AND INWARD PRODUCTIVITY—WHAT'S THE DIFFERENCE?

Are you resting enough or are you overworked? If you are currently overworked, I'd encourage you to reflect and discover why. If you're feeling overworked at your job, are there tasks that could be delegated to another person? If you're feeling overworked at home, could you ask your loved one for some help or outsource a task such as cleaning?

'I'll rest when I'm dead' is not a mantra to live by. If you constantly go from task to task, you'll become burnt out. According to Tania Diggory—founder of Calmer— burnout is 'the loss of meaning in one's work, coupled with mental, emotional, or physical exhaustion as the result of long-term, unresolved stress.'[12] Having experienced burnout firsthand, it is not something I recommend. Rest is an essential part of life and we need it in order to perform at our best. With technology making us available 24/7, it can be difficult to know when to shut off. I know I've been in job roles where my mind is racing even after I've walked out of the office, I've answered emails on my days off, and I've been stressed about what I'll walk into when I return. It's not easy finding a balance, and depending on the organisational culture, it may be the norm to work even after you've clocked off. It's crucial that you create boundaries to ensure you are not working all the time. You don't want to get to the point where you're not sleeping well because you're filled with anxiety or waiting for your phone to ring.

If you're constantly bringing work home, then you may want to consider setting boundaries by first monitoring how much you achieve during a workday. Are you procrastinating, spending too much time in meetings compared to doing your job, or are you spread too thin? By monitoring what tasks you do or don't do, as well the time spent doing each task, you can begin to identify patterns and places to improve. In some instances, you may be trying to do too many tasks that aren't essential to your role. It may be worthwhile having a conversation with your boss to clarify what tasks are essential and which ones could be assigned to others. If you do have a conversation, I'd recommend writing a list and having an idea of what tasks you believe are an integral part of your role to ensure you are sharing perspectives.

The above paragraphs relate to outer productivity. If you're constantly being outwardly productive without incorporating any in inwardly productive time in your day, then you may become burnt out over time. If you're feeling like you have to be productive all the time, I'd encourage you to check in with yourself and see how you feel. If you're feeling exhausted, it may be time to take a step back and begin to incorporate some inwardly productive time into your days.

Outer productivity refers to the tasks we complete. These tasks may be work-related or include attending events, helping out others, doing chores around the house, exercising, and so forth. It's the tasks that we do which yield a result.

Then there's inner productivity. When we are focusing on inner productivity, we are essentially finding ways to recharge our mind, body, and spirit. It's about discovering ways to relax and recharge. If you are accustomed to being on the go constantly, it will take time to adjust to this type of productivity. I realised I had spent years feeling like I had to be busy all the time after Jesse called me out on it. I'm glad he did, because now I've spent the past few years trying to incorporate a little more self-care and inner productivity time into my days.

At first, you may resist it. You may even be tempted to avoid it by getting distracted by doing another task. I know it will feel uncomfortable at first, but stick with it. View it as an appointment with yourself and hold yourself accountable to sticking to it rather than cancelling it. Give yourself permission to be inwardly productive and know that is an opportunity for you to recharge and it does not mean you are being lazy.

We all relax in different ways. I enjoy having a bath, going for a walk, reading, or listening to a webinar. I find each of these activities relaxing, but Jesse uses his relaxation time to play computer games. Find what works for you. The length of time is up to you: thirty minutes may be enough, or you may want to have a relaxation day. Listen to your body; some days you need more time to recharge your soul and mind.

It may take time to change your mindset in terms of how you view downtime if you're someone who likes to lead a full life. When you feel doubt, guilt, or any other negative emotion creeping in, take a moment to tell yourself that it's restorative and you're improving yourself. Just as when we're unwell we are told to rest, when we lead a full life we need to take a moment to relax. When we take time to focus on our inner self we can perform at a higher level.

If you're stuck for ideas, why not try some of the following and reflect on how you feel after each one? If it doesn't work, then try something else.

- Nature walk
- Reading
- Watching a movie/documentary/TV show
- Cooking
- Gardening
- Having a nap
- Lying under a tree
- Going for a drive
- Having a picnic
- DIY project
- Video game
- Listening to music
- Bubble bath

Chapter 17

IDENTIFYING THE WAY YOU WORK

E ach of us works differently. Some prefer a messier desk while others prefer a neat working space. Some prefer quiet spaces while others thrive in an open-plan office. The same applies when it comes to how we approach our tasks. I don't believe that there's a one-size-fits-all approach when it comes to implementing a time management strategy. Some of us thrive when there's a deadline looming, while others prefer to complete a task before the deadline. Then there's procrastination, and quite often it's used as an avoidance technique rather than one which increases productivity.

It's important to understand how you operate, because if you're currently working in a way that doesn't enable you to focus or perform at your best, you're essentially hindering your own performance. I understand that not all of us have the option of having our own office and we may not be able to ask our bosses to renovate the office, however, we can make changes to the way we approach our tasks.

Do you tend to complete tasks in advance so you know it's done, or do you put it off until the last minute? Furthermore, if you do leave it until the last minute, do you feel like you've achieved your best work, or has it been rushed and stressful? There are no right or wrong answers to any of these questions—it's simply an opportunity for you to learn more about the way you operate. Personally, I prefer to get tasks completed ahead of time because I don't like the stress that comes with a looming deadline. I know I don't perform at my best under negative stress and it shows in my work. However, if I am unsure of how to begin a task, I will procrastinate, and it's often under the false pretence that I'm waiting for inspiration to come to me.

Like me, your answer to the above questions may vary depending on the task. I find it easier to complete simple tasks straight away, but if it's a task that takes a while or that I'm unsure of, I am more likely to procrastinate. If you excel at tackling easy tasks straight away but put off larger and more complex tasks, consider breaking it down into smaller parts. Once you've broken it down into the smaller pieces, schedule time to work on each part. You could break down a two-hour task into four thirty-minute blocks instead—just as an example. It may be easier to allocate thirty minutes over a few days to get the task done rather than allocate two hours on a single day.

Doing a small part over time will get the task down. Work your way up to 100%. If it's not a task you can finish in a day, accept this and allocate a reasonable amount of time over a few days (or weeks or months, depending on the size of the task/project) to get it done. I think it's also important to acknowledge that there are times when we have to complete tasks that we really have no interest in doing. If we're lucky, we can delegate these tasks to others and focus on other priorities. However, there will be times when we aren't able to do that and we need to find a way to complete it ourselves. When your motivation is low, take action. When you take action, you build momentum and then motivation appears.

Make a plan, hold yourself accountable, and try not to make excuses. If you find yourself avoiding a task or procrastinating, check in with yourself and identify why you're avoiding the task. Find a method that works for you and enables you to perform at your best. Think about how you will feel once the task has been completed compared to the feelings of stress and anxiety that you may currently be experiencing. Once it's done, it can be ticked off the list and is no longer playing on your mind.

If you're someone who thrives under pressure and a looming deadline, kudos. If you're working in a team, let others know the way you work. If you're working on a task by yourself, you may still want to let others know how you work in case they want a progress report. If they know how you work, they will trust you to get it done and not be nervous if you haven't made any progress a few days out from the deadline.

Lastly, determine whether procrastination helps you to thrive or whether it hinders your performance. If it hinders your performance, remind yourself that when you are avoiding a task which needs to be completed, you are losing time and energy fretting about it. Instead, use that same time and energy to get it done. Less worrying, more doing.

Ask yourself:

1. Do you procrastinate?
2. How does it make you feel when you leave tasks to the last minute?
3. When do you perform your best?
4. Is there a pattern to your procrastination?

Chapter 18

HOW BUSYNESS
HINDERS CREATIVITY

Do you ever look at your calendar and feel overwhelmed by how many things are on it? I know I have. We are living through the COVID–19 pandemic. During this time, most of our schedules got wiped clean of events and social interactions. When the lockdowns first came into effect during the pandemic, I was sad. Jesse and I had to postpone our wedding, move our honeymoon, and a trip I had planned with my mum and sister had to be cancelled with one days' notice. It's fair to say that we have all experienced our own highs and lows as a result of the virus and now many of us are waiting to see what the new normal is going to look like.

If I were asked to find a positive during this time, it would be that it gave me a much-needed reprieve from being constantly busy. All the events that had filled up my calendar were removed, and I found myself with something precious—free time.

I was able to have space to breathe and to work on projects and activities that made me feel good. Through stillness (due to the space forced upon me), my creative spark was reignited. It was in this stillness that I was able to focus my attention on creative outlets again, something I hadn't made time for previously. Another opportunity that this time afforded me was time to reflect on what mattered to me. I decided to reflect on how I spent my time and how I was investing my energy. Once the lockdown restrictions eased, did I want to go back to the way life was (fitting multiple things into each weekend and feeling tired at the start of a work week?) or did I want to make change?

I've chosen to be more conscious of how I use my time. I no longer want to be busy being busy; instead, I want to make time for stillness and allow my creative spark to thrive. I've discovered that creativity requires stillness and moments free of noise in order for it to blossom.

If you want to allow creativity to be present in your life, give yourself permission to be still. Stillness may look different for you than it does to another. Personally, stillness is intertwined with solitude and being present. I find stillness while I am going for a walk or hike in nature, walking along the beach, having a bath, or practising yoga or meditation. Not only am I allowing my mind to stop racing and enjoy the present moment, but I am also giving my body the chance to rest or—when I choose to go for a walk—I am allowing myself to become energised. You may find stillness in other ways. Whatever your way, it's important that you give yourself time to be in this place of stillness to recharge, to get away from the white noise, and to be at one with your thoughts.

Many of us spend our days being busy for the sake of it. Our days are often filled with non-essential tasks. In some instances, this is a way for us to avoid boredom or having to be still with our thoughts. We avoid ourselves, our emotions, and as a result, we limit our ability to be creative.

When our days are continuously filled with back-to-back meetings, chores, and tasks, creativity cannot thrive. We are not giving ourselves space to be creative. Our minds need to rest so they can process information and make meaning of all the data they have received. When our brains are constantly being stimulated with new information and stimuli, you cannot generate creative ideas. Take a moment to reflect on when you last had an epiphany, revelation, or creative thought—chances are it was in a quiet moment. Stillness fosters creativity while busyness hinders it.

Between longer working days and advances in technology, we have the ability to fill free moments. If you're used to doing something all the time, you may struggle with stillness at first. It may feel uncomfortable because it's something out of the ordinary. In these moments, sit with your thoughts and notice how you feel. If you're feeling restless or bored, continue to sit there. Allow yourself the chance to be still and block out the white noise.

If you have ever tried frantically to find a set of keys or piece of jewellery that wasn't where you left it, you will likely know that you found it when you stopped looking. It's as if the item magically reappeared. When we get frantic and focus so strongly on trying to find something, whether it be an object, an answer, or an idea, it likely won't appear.

It isn't until you step back, clear your mind, or seek another perspective that the answer will come to you.

This is exactly how stillness and creativity works. When our minds are still, our subconscious is often thinking of an answer. Whether it be the closing line to a speech, the wording of a sales pitch that will allow you to close the deal, or the next sentence of your book when writers' block has taken over, stillness is the antidote.

Ask yourself:

1. Do you have any practices to foster creativity?
2. Where do you usually have your big ideas?
3. What does stillness look like to you?

Chapter 19

JUST THREE THINGS

Life has its ebbs and flows. Sometimes we have quiet days, weeks, or months. And yet, at other times our calendars are overflowing with looming deadlines, events, and appointments. It is when we are continuously in a state of being busy for prolonged periods of time that we may find ourselves feeling overworked, stressed, and overwhelmed.

Sometimes, it's unavoidable and you just need to take care of business. It's called the 'grind' for a reason. It's a challenging time, and when you have to spend most of your time, energy, and sometimes money on getting something completed such as launching a start-up, running a business, or meeting a deadline, it can be daunting. Self-care rituals may get taken off the calendar, your sleep patterns are disrupted, and the sense of work-life balance may also go out the window. If you exist in this state of being for a prolonged period of time, you can reach burnout, and from someone who has experienced burnout, I'd urge you not to reach this point. Be proactive and schedule in some self-care where you can.

Whether you're in the grind or just have a full schedule, take a moment to think of what is most important to you. Consider the things you can do each day which will give you a sense of accomplishment. Instant gratification can help when you are in the grind because 'micro-wins' can help keep you focused and on the path to achieving your end goal. It also takes the pressure off you because you know that if you do these things, you will feel like you accomplished something regardless of how the rest of the day went. We cannot do everything all at once. Trust me: I've tried that, and it doesn't work. You end up doing a little bit of many things rather than completing anything. Alternatively, you may try to fit too much into your day and when it's not all done, you feel as though you have let yourself down.

If you feel like you're not making progress, I'd encourage you to try a different approach. Try to be realistic with your time and what is possible in one day. Focus on just three things instead. I like to call it the 'three things' approach. Each day, choose three things that you want to achieve for that day. If you can do more than this, great! But these three things are at the core of your to do list, and once they're done, you can go to sleep and rest easy because you did those things. I find this is especially helpful when you have a habit of trying to cram too much into a day. It helps you take a step back and evaluate what really matters to you that day. They don't even need to be work-related or productive. They could be spending time with loved ones, going for a walk, and watching your favourite TV show.

Plan your time and place a high value on it. Time is the one commodity which none of us can replenish. Once it's used, it's gone forever. If you're feeling anxious or stressed about the day, give yourself time to plan and work out how you will approach the day. Try to begin each day in a calm state rather than feeling stressed and overwhelmed. I know it's not always possible because some days are busier than others, but on these days, check in and confirm with yourself what your three things are.

You can use the table below as an example way of recording your three things. You can keep it super simple and just write a list with three dot points with a task next to each of them, but if you're wanting to be more mindful of why you're choosing this task, you can write that down as well.

It's okay for your lists to be different on a daily basis. Some days you may feel like making larger tasks a priority, while other days, it may be something smaller. It doesn't matter, provided that whatever you write down and complete leaves you feeling like you achieved something today. The point is to reduce our stress, anxiety, and feelings of frustration which often come as a result of feeling like we haven't done enough in a day.

Task	Why I want to achieve it	Complete

You're holding yourself accountable by writing a list. You're setting an intention for your day, and let's face it, who doesn't love seeing a list that's completed in full? If you use the table above, you'll also know why you want to achieve it and you'll feel good when you can mark it as done.

Celebrate the completion of this list each day. Do not feel guilty if that's all you do in a day. It is more than doing nothing, which can happen on days when we're feeling overwhelmed and don't know where to begin. This can help you to overcome procrastination and breakdown your to-do list and larger goals into smaller, doable pieces.

Ask yourself:

1. Create a large daily to-do list.
2a. Then create a smaller 'three things you can do today' list.
2b. Once you have accomplished your three things, reflect on how you feel and write that down.
3. Think of how you feel when you complete a small list compared to a larger list. Does a smaller list make you want to accomplish items on it more than the other?

Chapter 20

THE BENEFITS OF IMPLEMENTING A 'POWER HOUR'

As adults, our to-do lists seem to get longer and longer. Tasks get pushed aside because something more important comes up. As a result, some of these tasks may take weeks, months, or even years to attend to. Incomplete tasks have a tendency to weigh us down as we spend time and energy thinking of when we can accomplish them. This can lead to feeling stressed and overwhelmed.

When Jesse and I first moved in together, it was an exciting time. Jesse built a house, which meant we had to pack and unpack but also do a lot of work around the house. From furnishing to deciding on a back yard design and painting the house, it felt like a never-ending list of things to do. Both of us have full-time jobs so it meant that for the foreseeable future, our weekends were dedicated to making the house a home. When it came to painting the house, it felt overwhelming. Not only did we need to choose colours, but we had to clean the walls and paint multiple coats. We ended up painting on weeknights for an hour or so after work to try to get it done. By allocating small pockets of time to a larger task, we were able to make steady progress without feeling obliged to paint for an entire weekend.

This is where the 'power hour' comes in. It's an hour that can be allocated to completing one of those nagging tasks. Depending on the size of the task, you may be able to complete more than one, or if it's a larger project, you can get a part of it done. If this approach resonates with you, create a separate to do list and call it your 'power hour tasks'.

When it comes to the more complex tasks, we push them to the side, telling ourselves we will do them another day, then another day comes and we push them aside, and so it continues on. It also means that if a task comes up and it's not urgent, then you can consider allocating it to that week or following week's power hour itinerary so you know it will get done.

If you want more accountability, you can always schedule a power hour with your loved one, a friend, or family member. Then, each of you can accomplish something without the guilt of not spending time together. Even if you aren't able to do a power hour item together, you still have something to share and celebrate when you reconnect.

If you're not able to complete the full power hour at first, you can always try thirty minutes. When you are trying to build a habit or add something new into your schedule, be kind and patient with yourself. It takes time to implement. The main thing is to schedule it and hold yourself accountable. As with many things, it can be easy to take it off the schedule. I'd challenge you to try it once and see how you feel after.

Chances are it'll be a feeling similar to when you go the gym. Before you go, your mind goes through the standard excuses as to why you can't go or tries to negotiate, such as 'I won't go today but I'll go tomorrow instead.' But, when you push through these thoughts and work out, you feel better afterwards. It's hard to find someone who regrets a work-out. Exercise releases endorphins and gives you an energy boost. While completing a task which has been on your to do list for a while may not give you the same energy boost, it will free up space in your mind.

If we apply this same process to trying a power hour to work through the tasks we put off, then we get to feel the satisfaction that comes with removing it from the list for good. You remind yourself what you can achieve, and by allocating an hour to it, you hold yourself accountable. Focus your energy on the task and see if it can be done or at least started.

Ask yourself:

1. Write a list for your power hour tasks.
2. Clump smaller tasks together and break larger tasks down into actionable pieces.
3. Schedule the power hour during the week.

Chapter 21

WHAT DO YOU WANT FROM A JOB?

Some people build their lives around work, while others prefer to have a job which allows them freedom and the ability to switch off at the end of each workday. If you're currently in a job which you've outgrown or have stayed in longer than you should have, it's worthwhile thinking about what you want from a job. Even if you're content with your current position, it is still a good activity to do.

To begin, ask yourself this question: what need do you want your job to fill? Is it enough for you to have a job that allows you to cover your daily expenses, or would you prefer a job that also leaves you with some disposable income? Do you want a job that enables you to progress and grow, or are you content having a job with less responsibility and being able to leave work at work? Do you want a job that gives you a sense of purpose? Do you want to work part-time or full-time? There are many questions you can ask yourself and you may want to use a journal to write down what comes to mind.

If you're unsure of what you want from your job, you can always start with what you don't want. By using the process of elimination, you can understand what you *do* want. It may be that you don't want a job that involves travel, shift work, or weekend work. You could even think of what you don't want in terms of the organisational culture and workspace. You may prefer to have flexible working hours and a short commute. Once you start narrowing down the parameters, the answers will soon begin to reveal themselves to you.

Is it job security? Is it the job title? Is it the responsibility or flexibility to dictate your hours and how you complete the tasks? Once you've written down a list of what you do or don't want from a job, it's time for the next step. It's time to evaluate your current situation.

Full disclaimer: I don't believe there's such a thing as the perfect job; however, your job shouldn't make you miserable or burnt out. Previously, I have worked for a company which didn't align with my core values and another which led me to become burnt out; I understand how challenging it can be to have a job that drains you of your energy. Considering how much each of us spends working during our lives, it's crucial that we find a job that we enjoy doing.

If you have compared what you do and don't want in a job to your current situation and have discovered that there's a discrepancy, you may want to ask yourself another question: is it repairable or do I need to find another job? It may be that you're ready to change careers or become an entrepreneur.

I don't endorse resigning without a contingency plan unless, of course, you are the kind of soul who likes to wing it, and if that's you, do what feels right. When I first entered the workforce, my dad instilled some wisdom in me and that was to never resign without having another job lined up beforehand. There was one job when I was ready to resign, effective immediately, but I didn't. I waited until I had secured another job and then I resigned. I like knowing that I have something to move on to rather than scrambling trying to find another job, even if I know it will only be temporary. That being said, I know we are in different situations and you may not have any other choice than to leave if that workplace is toxic for you. In that case, if it's possible, I'd still encourage you to try to save some money just so you can still live while you're looking for your next thing.

There's so much change in the job space that the concept of choosing a career and sticking with it until you retire is long-gone for most of us. We have the ability to work in different roles and see what we enjoy. You are not stuck where you are, and if you're unhappy, you can do something about it. Just remember that playing the victim is not going to change your situation. Take action instead.

Chapter 22

THE IMPORTANCE OF HAVING A HOBBY

A hobby is an activity which is done regularly during your recreational or leisure time. It is an activity which brings pleasure rather than monetary gain. Having a hobby is a meaningful way to spend your leisure time. Hobbies can include creative and artistic activities, sporting activities, collecting items, and building things. You may even classify learning or reading as a hobby as well.

Whether you're single or in a relationship, having a hobby is beneficial because it adds to your self-identity. As a bonus, you get the opportunity to spend your time doing something which 'fills your cup' and is for you. Not all hobbies need to transform into side-hustles or a full-time job—they can simply be a part of your life for the purpose of bringing you joy. The value that you place on a hobby is up to you. One of my long term hobbies is photography. I am a beginner, but I truly enjoy capturing moments and sharing them with loved ones. When I haven't taken photos for a while, I notice a subtle change in my mood, but as soon as I'm back behind the lens, I feel a lift in my spirit again. Hobbies provide us with an outlet to immerse ourselves in activity that brings us great joy.

Hobbies are fantastic for a number of reasons:

- You can meet like-minded people.
- You can develop a skill.
- You'll have a topic for conversation.
- You can keep your brain stimulated.
- It can be part of a self-care routine.
- You can exert creative energy.
- They provide a sense of joy and/or accomplishment.

There isn't a one-size-fits-all approach to hobbies. What may bring pleasure to one person may not to you. For instance, Jesse likes to spend time gaming on his computer with friends. It is an activity that lights him up but it's not one that interests me. Try not to put pressure on yourself when looking for a hobby. It's an activity to do for yourself rather than others.

As children, we are often encouraged to pursue various hobbies, but as adults, we tend to neglect our interests. While for short periods of time life may be full and it may not be possible to allocate time to a hobby, it should still be something to schedule time for as regularly as possible. Work, children, volunteering, studying, and so forth can reduce your leisure time. If you want to make time to focus on a hobby, trust you can do it. Start by making it a priority and do an audit to see what you are spending your time on which is non-essential.

Is there an activity you used to enjoy but you haven't done for a while? Is it because you outgrew it, found another hobby, or ran out of time? If it's because you're feeling time-poor, I'd encourage you to look at where you are spending your time. Write out a detailed list for the week to see where your time is going. Chances are there is room for a hobby, if you are willing to make it a priority and spend less time on another thing. Determine whether there are non-essential tasks you are spending time on which you could let go of or delegate to others. For instance, you could start to have your groceries delivered to you rather than spending two hours at the shops each week. We get caught up in thinking that being busy is good, so we fill our days to the brim and are busy being busy rather than curating a life which brings us joy, happiness, and a sense of purpose.

Brené Brown made a point during her discussion with Oprah on the *SuperSoul Conversations* podcast when she stated that unused creativity doesn't become benign; rather, it transforms into negative emotions.[13] This statement reinforces the importance of having a creative outlet and the impact—positive or negative—that it has on our mental wellbeing. When we are trying to become the best version of ourselves, low-level emotions (such as anger, sadness, or frustration) can hinder our progress. So, consider taking up a hobby as an investment in improving your mental health.

When I heard that, it truly resonated with me. When I was younger, my mum, sister, and I would often do craft projects at home and, while I may not have been great at every project we attempted, I had a lot of fun. But once I made it through high school and transitioned into young adult and now adult stage, I didn't allow time for these projects. It wasn't until the middle of 2018 that I realised I wanted to start doing craft projects again and my mood began to improve. Why? I had an outlet to release my creative energy rather than letting it be buried. Even if it's only thirty minutes or an hour per week that you can allocate to your hobby, it can have still have a positive impact on your mental health over time.

Ask yourself:

If you haven't had a hobby for a while and aren't sure what you might be interested in, ask yourself any of the following questions:

1. What hobbies did I have during my childhood?
2. If I had a day to spend how I wanted, what would I do?
3. Is there a hobby that my friends or family have that interests me?
4. Is there an event or workshop I want to attend?
5. What topics am I interested in?
6. Look at meet up pages, volunteering, or community forums for inspiration.
7. Is there a friend or family member who you can invite to go with you?

Chapter 23

INTENTION

Vision without action is merely a dream. Action without vision just passes the time. Vision with action can change the world.
—JOEL ARTHUR BAKER

Setting an intention for your day is a powerful practice to build into your daily routine. While we cannot control our day in its entirety and it may not go exactly how we envisioned it to, that doesn't mean we are powerless. You can be mindful of what you would like your day to look like. We can do this by creating an intention of how we would like to conduct ourselves each day and the tasks we would like to attend to.

Intentions don't need to be elaborate. It's a practice that encourages you to pause before you begin your day to think about the kind of day you would ideally like to have and the energy you would like to give and attract. You can also visualise yourself moving with ease throughout each part of your day. Setting an intention for your day helps you to become present and consider what you would like to do. Just as making a plan doesn't guarantee everything will run as planned, neither does an intention. There may be days when you intended to get a certain activity completed, but something comes up. Rather than getting attached to your intention, see it as a guiding light rather than an absolute that must be adhered to strictly.

The day can either control us or we can control it, to some degree. You have the power to decide how you would like to approach each day. Many times, we choose to give our power to external forces, allowing social media and planned schedules to dictate our time and, in turn, how we react. While it may seem simpler to go with the flow, and at times it can be, you have the power to determine how you lead your life, starting with each day. If you want to start setting an intention for each day, take a few moments to think about the day ahead when you wake up. Alternatively, you can set your intention for the following day the night before, depending on what feels right for you.

When setting your intention, consider:

- Do you have a full day, or is it a day of rest?
- Who will you be spending time with?
- Will you be leaving the house or staying in?
- How much time will you allocate to your self-care rituals? When will you complete them?
- How are you feeling about this day?
- What are top three priorities for the day?

If you have a full day ahead, then you may want to set the intention to take a break between tasks to check in with yourself for a minute of mindful breathing. Or you could set the intention to be joyful and live in the moment if you're celebrating a special occasion. Intentions don't need to be fixed; they can change daily, weekly, or monthly, depending on how you feel and the day ahead. Just as we change our clothes to suit the season, your intention can change to suit your day. So, make the choice to dress accordingly.

We are in control of how we behave and react to situations and our environment. If you intend to act with kindness and compassion, then make an intention which enables you to embody those values. You can consider giving a compliment to a loved one, a perfect stranger, or colleague and be kind when interacting with those around you.

When I first began my gratitude practice, I found it easier to list three things I was grateful for on a day off. On workdays, I struggled to find things to be grateful for. If you're like me in this regard, you could try to seek out things to be grateful for. You could be grateful for a well-made coffee, a relaxing lunch break, or an activity after work. Being grateful for life's simple pleasures can make life extraordinary.

Ask yourself:

1. Focus on your energy: what energy do you want to bring with you throughout the day and will this change depending on where you are?

2. Focus on your time: can you schedule time to take a break between meetings/tasks to refocus?

3. Focus on self-care: what activities, habits or tasks will you complete and when?

4. Focus on your values: how do you want to incorporate your value/s into your interactions with others?

5. When will you allocate time to work on your goals?

Chapter 24

YOU ARE NOT YOUR THOUGHTS

Your thoughts are not the absolute truth. We can either let our thoughts control us, or we can control them. Just because we think something doesn't mean it is true or needs to be dwelt upon.

If you allow your negative thoughts to control you, you may become paralysed and stuck where you are. Over time you confine yourself to the walls you built around yourself. Our inner dialogue often likes to remind us of our perceived flaws and weaknesses, trying to convince us that playing small or not trying is better than taking risks and growing. While there are good intentions behind such thoughts, they can hinder our performance if we continually buy into our fear-based thoughts.

Thoughts are fleeting; they come and go. Just as we breathe, we think. When we hold on to our inhalation, we eventually have to exhale; it cannot last forever. But when it comes to our thoughts, we hold on to them, some for longer than what is needed. We wouldn't hold onto our breath until we ran out of air, so why do we do this with our thoughts?

When a thought lingers, it is because you have given the thought power and allowed it to control how you act. Remember: what you think, you become. It is up to you how you engage with your thoughts and which ones you simply acknowledge and let go of. Not all thoughts are worth holding on to, especially when they are self-limiting or ego-based.

We can allow fear, anger, sorrow, hurt, and pain to manifest in our minds, and ultimately in different areas of our lives, or we can acknowledge these thoughts as they come, and then let them go. If you want to become your ultimate self, you may need to consider how you engage with your thoughts. Do you allow your inner voice to glide over the positive thoughts and dwell on the negative, or do you focus on the positive thoughts more?

Not every day is the same. Some days you may find it effortless to notice your thoughts come and go, but other days it may be more challenging. When I first started practising this technique (of observing my thoughts), I was surprised by what I was thinking. Many ideas were repeated daily, such as, *It's time for coffee,* as well as thoughts about my appearance. Do your best on that day rather than comparing each practice to the previous ones. When a thought comes to the forefront of your mind, question the thought and make a conscious decision about whether you will discard it or listen to it. If we think of our minds as an email inbox and our thoughts as messages, we can create a filtering system to determine what is deemed as spam and what we will act on. With time, our filters get more personalised and it will be easier to determine which thoughts are worthy of your time and which ones are not.

Approach your thoughts with grace and compassion. To embody grace is to think and act with compassion, love, and kindness. It is acceptance of ones' self, others, and the situation. Rather than acting out of fear or judgement or striving for perfectionism, accept the situation as it is and say to yourself: 'and so it is'. Regain control over your thoughts. Separate yourself from your thoughts and know that just because you thought it, it doesn't make it true.

If you find that you have difficulty letting go of fearful thoughts, or that they are impacting your life negatively, please contact a medical professional.

Chapter 25

OVERCOMING OUR NEGATIVITY BIAS

Our brains have an in-built negativity bias. While we may not be able to completely remove the bias, we can train our brain to look for the positives. We can do this by changing the language we use and how we approach and respond to situations.

The language we use matters. Words can have a positive or negative effect on you, and many have an emotion attached to the word. Let's begin with the way we talk to ourselves. How many of your thoughts about yourself are positive compared to the negative ones? My guess is that negative thoughts outweigh the positive. Rather than allowing our negative thoughts to take over, we can catch the thought and flip it. Turn the negative into a positive. Instead of saying, 'I look okay in this outfit,' say, 'I am rocking this outfit.' You deserve to love the person you are and who you are becoming unconditionally. Negative self-talk doesn't support this loving relationship, so if you are thinking negatively about yourself, try to catch the thought, flip it, and notice the difference it has on you. Feeling confident and happy with who you are isn't egotistical, it's just about embracing who you are and knowing that you are enough as you are.

The way we talk to ourselves isn't limited to just our appearance—it's also about how we conduct ourselves. When you have made a mistake, be accountable and don't feel ashamed, stupid, or incompetent. You are only human, and we all make mistakes. Learn from it and let it go. As many of us know, it's much easier to put yourself down than it is to pull yourself up, but with time and practice, it gets easier. Another example is instead of apologising for being late, you can thank the person for waiting. Save your apologies for when it's needed. Sometimes we say sorry as a reflex and it loses its worth. By saying 'thank you for waiting,' you acknowledge that the person was waiting for you and that you appreciate their patience. 'Sorry' implies you have done something wrong, while 'thank you' signifies appreciation. Change your language and notice the difference in the person's response and body language (if you're in person).

Some people adore winter while others get the winter blues. If you feel down during the cooler months, find ways to celebrate the season. While you may not want to go for walks or runs in the rain, you can spend time indoors with loved ones, work on projects, and recharge. Rain can bring rainbows, greener crops, and help farmers grow fresh produce which we love to consume. Sure, it may limit our ability to bask in the sunlight, but we can find other ways of occupying our time. Plus, it means wearing cosy clothes and having wholesome and hearty meals.

When you're having a challenging day, you can fall into the trap of finding things that justify your mood. Some days we just wake up on the wrong side of the bed and it seems as though the world is against us. You may have slept through your alarm, got caught in traffic, or someone may not have done the work they were meant to, and so forth. If we go through the day in a grumpy mood, we attract that energy back to us. Each moment we have a choice of how we conduct ourselves. We can choose to be grumpy at something that happened a few hours before or we can let it go and try to have a better day. If you're finding it difficult to shake off a bad mood, stop and consciously do something that is bound to make you smile. While we can't go from sad to happy in an instant, we can gradually improve our mood.

If you're wanting to improve your mood, take a minute and take a few deep breaths. When you concentrate on your breathing, you become grounded and focus back on the current moment. If you're able to look or go outside, take a quick walk and look around you. What do you see? What can you hear? What can you feel? Alternatively, give someone a sincere compliment, show kindness, or do a good deed for another. Make sure you are being genuine though, otherwise the inauthenticity won't do much to improve your mood. If you're mad or frustrated, try going for a short walk and getting out of the environment. If you break free of the situation—even for a few minutes—you can get out of your head and begin to think clearly again. If you're a words person, try saying 'bubbles'—chances are you cannot say it with a frown or grimaced teeth.

Alternatively, you can review your daily routine. Create rituals which leave you feeling empowered and comfortable in your own skin. Below are some activities which bring me a sense of joy, and while they work for me, they may not for you. Don't be afraid to experiment and see what works for you. I like to think of them as positivity boosters because these activities make me feel better regardless of the mood I was in beforehand. Your list may look different to mine and that's fine, I'm just sharing what works for me to give you a starting point.

- Having a bath.
- Going for a walk.
- Hanging out with Jesse or the dog.
- Listening to a podcast.
- Cooking.
- Reading a book.
- Dancing or singing to a favourite song.
- Spending time with loved ones.
- Having a massage.
- Travelling.
- Doing something creative.

So, while we can't free ourselves completely of the negativity bias, we can search for the positive. Change your language, perspective, and actions to facilitate a more positive outlook.

While fake positivity isn't healthy, neither is being negative all the time. Feel your feelings, be aware of the thoughts and which ones you want to ponder and discard, and trust that you will feel better if you are able to find the positive.

Chapter 26

WHAT DO YOU BELIEVE?

If you want to attract something into your life, you need to put it out into the universe. What you reflect, you attract. It may not be instantaneous, but the universe has a way of providing opportunities which reflect your thoughts. If you want to improve an aspect of your life such as your social connections, you need to believe that you are deserving of this.

It may be the introvert in me, but I've always been a firm believer in quality over quantity when it comes to friendships. I'd rather have a small group of friends who I know well and vice versa than have a large quantity of friends. We are all different, and if you're a social butterfly, spread your wings and fly! As an adult, my circle of friends is almost non-existent, and this is due to a few reasons:

1. I do not believe I am worthy of friends,
2. I do not know why someone would want to be my friend, and
3. I don't spend time socialising or networking at events or gatherings I do attend.

It's easy to say the reason why I don't have many friends is because I'm an introvert but that's not entirely true. I say I want more friends and to meet new people and make connections, and yet my actions and self-beliefs do not reflect this. Words without action are simply words. It goes deeper than being an introvert: it is the belief that I am not worthy of having friends.

This belief stemmed from being bullied as a kid throughout school. I did try to work through this when I was in my senior years of school and beyond, but I haven't let go of the baggage completely. I believe that I am not deserving of friends, and as a result I have limited friendships. Being bullied led me to create a false truth: that I wasn't worthy of having true friends. This belief has blocked my ability to make new friendships, because deep down I don't feel worthy. Fortunately, thanks to the help of Jesse and some introspection, I am beginning to realise that I am deserving and people who I consider as acquaintances, I could actually call a friend.

It's not easy when you have damaging self-beliefs, but if we carry these false truths with us, then we limit our ability to improve our situation moving forward. If we don't believe that we are worthy of love, wealth, happiness, good health, a long life, friends, romance, et cetera, then chances are we won't receive this. It is only once we realise our own self-worth and believe we are worthy that these parts of our lives will begin to improve.

Perhaps you have your own version of events which have led you to limiting yourself in aspects of your life due to your beliefs. So, the question is, what do you believe you are worthy of? What do you believe you don't deserve or aren't worthy of? Once you have taken time to reflect on both of these questions, you may have a better understanding of why some aspects of your life have stagnated, and while you may seek to improve them, it isn't working. If you don't believe you are worthy of love, you will allow yourself to either be single or fall in and out of relationships that are not meant for you. Once you change your belief, the universe will rise to meet you. When we feel inadequate, we are limiting our own ability to thrive in this area of our life.

Belief is valuable: it gives you hope for the future, faith that things will work out, and it allows you to work in the present. As we know, life doesn't always go according to plan, but if we limit ourselves by a lack of self-belief, we are not allowing the universe to provide us with opportunities. We close the door before it has even opened.

Ask yourself:

1. What do you believe to be true?
2. What self-limiting beliefs do you have?
3. Where do these beliefs come from?
4. What do you believe will be in your future?
5. What thoughts are holding you back?

Chapter 27

MEDITATION

Meditation can assist you in manifesting your goals and dreams, notice your thoughts, calm your mind, and help you to find peace. It allows you to be still for a few moments to reconnect with your body and mind. You can listen to your thoughts and body signals without distraction.

Surrender to how you feel in that moment without judgement. If you believe that you are more than your thoughts and your current situation and are capable of change, you can create a shift in your mood and how your body feels. You may want to consider incorporating meditation into your routine if you find that you have limited focus and get distracted easily when you're doing a task or if you're trying to find the off switch to calm a racing mind.

If meditation isn't something that you have tried before, it may take a while to get into a meditative state. Try not to get frustrated if you cannot calm your mind or focus solely on your breath. Each day is different and it's important to be kind to yourself. Accept that you did the best that you could for that day and try again tomorrow. There are many types of meditations so if one form of meditation doesn't work for you, keep trying different ones until you find one that does.

If sitting with your thoughts seems unnerving, you can begin with a short guided meditation. Guided meditations are good as the speaker will give you guidance on how to breathe, what to focus on, and how to accept your thoughts and let them go. Guided meditations can also focus on a certain topic such as setting an intention, reducing stress, doing a body scan, and so much more. Even if you meditate for a short amount of time, you will notice a difference. Remember to monitor your progress by having a journal to write down your thoughts and how you feel following each session, or you can just ask yourself once you have completed the practice. As meditation has become more popular, there are numerous guided meditations, soft songs, and other tools available to help you on your journey. The purpose of meditation is to achieve a feeling of mindfulness by being in touch with the present moment and the sensations of the body. Be kind to yourself as it will take time to get used to quietening your mind and listening to your body.

If you have a racing mind and find it challenging to sit still, you may feel frustrated if you're not seeing an immediate change in your mood or your ability to put your thoughts to the background and focus on the present moment. Be patient with yourself; just like with any new activity, it will take time to become better. To become a master, you must first be a student. Meditation gives you the chance to be, to accept your inner dialogue and any thoughts and to let them go. You can address these thoughts and other items on your schedule later, but for now, just allow yourself to experience the present moment. Forget the past and the future, and just be here in the now. When you do give yourself permission to stop and complete a meditation practice, be proud of yourself.

Meditation isn't necessarily about removing all thoughts from your mind, but rather being conscious of your thoughts and how your body feels. You can also use meditation as a way to tune into how you are feeling, setting an intention for the day, and manifesting. You may vary your practice depending on what you would like to achieve. Find what works for you. It's a personal practice so there is not a one-size-fits-all approach to follow.

I have practised meditation for a few years now. I've had times where it has been part of my daily routine consistently for a few months and then I take a step back. I may go weeks without meditating and then I will bring it back into my morning routine when I feel it's needed. I prefer to view meditation as a choice rather than a chore, which is why I don't force myself to mediate daily. I will do a short practice when I feel stressed or anxious as it helps to ground me. I still have days where I feel like I can't quieten my mind and I wrestle with the stillness, but it's on these days that I know I need it the most.

By allowing yourself to take some time to meditate, you are giving yourself permission to focus on you. Acknowledge your thoughts, breathe in, and notice points of tension, how you are feeling, and what intention you want to set for the day. For many of us who have a short attention span, you may also find you have a better ability to focus on tasks without being distracted or bored.

Use your senses in the moment. You can focus on your breath or finding certain items or colours in the space surrounding you. By focusing on one single item, it will bring you back into the present moment. This technique can be beneficial if you sense that you are distracted, thinking about another place and time, or stressed. It grounds you to the moment and forces your mind to become more still.

Meditation is a personal practice. If you aren't comfortable with sitting cross-legged or lying on the floor in stillness or listening to a guided meditation, you can find an activity which feels meditative for you. It could be going for a walk, a run, having a bath, practising yoga, or having some quiet reflective time without any distractions. It's about reconnecting with your mind and body in whatever form feels right for you.

Ask yourself:

1. Find a meditation to listen to, whether it be a song to play in the background or a guided meditation.
2. Find a space and allocate time to meditate (if you are a planner, schedule it).
3. Write down how you feel before and after you meditate.

Chapter 28

BE KIND

Kindness is an underrated virtue. It is often overlooked, and yet many of us appreciate it when others show us kindness and compassion. We can choose to act from a place of love and kindness or from a place of animosity.

On days when life gets ahead of us, we may feel tired, stressed, and anxious. When we have a short fuse or little patience, we often become abrupt and snappy. I know I've had moments where I've been rude to loved ones, and the worst part is that I know it's because I'm tired and I just don't have the mental energy to stop myself. When we are aware of how we feel, we can consciously decide how we will respond. We can make others aware of our mood, and if we aren't able to control our emotional response, we can always apologise and be accountable for our behaviour.

The secret to being a kind person to others is to not expect it in return. We cannot control the actions of others, only ourselves. We can choose to be kind or to be irate, just as others have that same choice. Many people who work in customer service roles will understand this. You have the power to decide how you engage with others, just as they have the choice of how they want to interact with you. If someone is being unkind, try not to take it personally and instead still show them kindness. Try not to change your behaviour to mirror that of another, especially if they're being impolite. It's not worth the effort.

Showing kindness to others costs us nothing, but it has a positive impact on someone else. It also makes you feel good when you are kind so the return on investment is much greater than being angry. There's no remorse, guilt, or sadness associated with being kind as there is if you're mad, angry, or frustrated. You can create a ripple effect of kindness by showing kindness to others. It's easy to yell at someone in person or over the phone, or to write an aggressive email when you are frustrated by someone or a situation, but before you react, consider the consequences. Is it worth the guilt and, even if the person was at fault, is it really worth getting upset over it?

When we get angry at others, whether it was personally their fault or not, we ruin our mood and potentially their mood as well. For those in customer service roles, kindness goes a long way. Something as simple as saying 'hello', 'please', and 'thank you' will go further than you think. Words are powerful. I remember when I used to work at a supermarket, and I would interact with people who were kind and then others who were impatient, irate, or angry. I always tried to go into work with a positive attitude, but some shifts would wear me down emotionally, especially if many people were impolite. Even when you try to not let it bother you or to take it personally, it still gets to you. As a result, I try my best to be kind, polite, and attentive when interacting with staff in such roles as I know that kindness goes further than being impolite. Just because you are having a tough day doesn't mean you have the right to ruin another's day.

Treat others with kindness as often as you can. Remember, we are not perfect beings, so if there is a time when you choose another emotion over kindness, let it go. If we are unable to accept and love our own flaws, we may be caught up in searching for flaws in others and using it against them. We try to change others, especially those closest to us, whether we are conscious of this or not, and then when they do change, we comment on this and use it as a reason to say goodbye. Rather than searching for the flaws, we can try to train our minds to search for the good. Just as gratitude can help us search for the beauty that surrounds us in each moment, we can search for the good in others. Elevate strengths rather than focusing on a weakness. When we focus on the good, we can build and find others who have strengths that we can complement.

If you want to think of ways to show kindness to others, some examples of simple acts of kindness include smiling, acknowledging someone else, or paying a compliment to someone.

Chapter 29

RESILIENCE

Life doesn't get easier or more forgiving;
we get stronger and more resilient.
—STEVE MARABOLI

esilience is about how we cope and bounce back from difficulties. As we know, life isn't always easy. No matter who you are, life has highs and lows. What differentiates us during the difficult times is how we respond to the situation. Do we become a victim, or do we actively try to find a solution? The answer depends on your level of resilience.

There will be times when life goes smoothly, and other times where this will not be the case. There will be setbacks and roadblocks, as well as internal and external doubt, especially if you are stepping out of your comfort zone. It's in the challenging times that you get to develop your levels of resilience. You have two options in such situations: you can throw your hands up and walk away or you can choose to continue. You have the power to choose what you do.

If you look at individuals who have achieved success, they put in the hard yards. The concept of being an overnight success is a myth. We tell ourselves that they've achieved success quickly and easily rather than acknowledging that their journey most likely took much longer. We only see the finished product or a skill that is often years in the making. We don't see the long nights, the hard decisions, and the blood, sweat, or tears that are behind the person or product. If such individuals didn't have high levels of resilience, we may not have seen what they were truly capable of. The same goes for you.

It's not only in business that we can begin to build up our levels of resilience; we can also become more resilient in other areas of our lives such as in our relationships. If someone hurts you, learn to let it go. Feel your way through the situation rather than let it define you. Call the person out and explain how it made you feel, or if it means letting go of a toxic relationship, know that you are strong enough to do so. Holding onto grudges or allowing situations to upset you for an extended period of time is not beneficial. You're investing time into a situation that has already happened and that negative energy is draining. When you're allowing something or someone to affect your mood, it's you who primarily suffers. Instead of feeling victimised and wondering why it happened to you, search for the lesson and overcome it.

Resilience is a skill, and like any skill, it can be developed over time with practice. Resilience is falling down seven times but standing up eight. It's about persevering and finding the silver lining. I don't believe resilience is about faking optimism; it's healthy to be realistic and admit when a situation hasn't gone as planned or to grieve when needed. It's about how you carry yourself during the smooth seas and how you adjust your sails when the seas get tough. As the saying goes, 'smooth seas don't make for a good sailor.' Rather than staying in the port, set sail and learn to navigate the waters. It's you how you learn and build your resilience. You can read about how to be more resilient, but until you put the theory into action, you won't know how resilient you truly are.

If you find yourself getting caught up in stress and unravelling if there's a slight delay, bump in the road, or an unexpected problem, you may want to start building on your current levels of resilience by approaching the situation from a different perspective. Rather than getting stressed and letting negative thoughts and emotions flood your brain and body, take a deep inhalation and let it go. Taking a few deep breaths allows you to return to the present moment. It shifts you from a state of stress to a state of calm. It is in this state that you can make a better decision. This allows you to look at the situation holistically and, hopefully, you begin to come up with solutions to the problem or find a silver lining. Remind yourself that 'there's a positive in every negative and a negative in every positive.' Situations happen *for* you and not *to* you. Look for the lesson.

For example, when you apply for the job or promotion only to find out you weren't successful, it's a blow to the system. Instead of allowing your inner voice to list 101 reasons why you didn't get the job—such as you're inadequate, you're not qualified, you blew the interview, and so forth—you can choose to focus on the positives. You can ask for constructive feedback to see if there is something you can improve on and then let it go. Trust that something better is coming.

Feedback can be a useful tool to help you identify any areas that you can work on if it's delivered in a constructive manner; however, you should not allow others to shape you. If the feedback is negative and does not serve you, smile and let it go. We each see life through our own lens and create our own views about a situation, topic, or person.

View the application process and interview as experience rather than as a failed attempt. You can use what you learnt to your advantage. You know that you have a resumé and/or cover letter that is attractive to potential employers, and the more interview experience you have, the better you'll be in future interviews. With practice comes reduced nerves: you know how to conduct yourself and you can just be yourself.

Trust that you did the best you could and move on. Sometimes there is a better candidate for the position, and while it may be disheartening that you didn't get the role, there are other jobs out there and you'll land the one that is right for you.

Ask yourself:

1. Write a list of three people that you consider to be resilient.
2. What situations trigger you to feel stressed, anxious, or frustrated? Why is that?
3. What are your known triggers and what steps can you take to reduce the effect it has on you?
4. Think of a situation which didn't have the outcome you were hoping for. How did you respond? How did you feel? What would a resilient person do in this situation?
5. Do you feel stuck when a situation doesn't go as planned, or do you seek out solutions?

Chapter 30

GRATITUDE

'Gratitude' is derived from the Latin word *gratus* which means 'thankful' or 'pleasing' (source: *Macmillan Dictionary*). It is a feeling that allows you to be thankful for all that you have rather than what may be lacking.

When you live in a state of gratitude, fear cannot rule your heart or mind. Fear and gratitude cannot coexist. By shifting your mind to focus each day on three things that brought you joy and happiness, or you were grateful for, it allows you to start subconsciously looking for the good in each moment.

We are spiritual beings having a physical experience. What we put out into the world (consciously or subconsciously), we will attract back. If you are looking for things to get irate about, you will find them. On the flipside, if you're searching for things to appreciate, you'll find these also. Whatever your thoughts, the universe will provide reasons to back you up. If you want to attract peace or gratitude, you must learn to transmit this. Radiate, manifest, and think this way. When you are in a state of gratitude your mind will find more reasons to be grateful. Living in a state of gratitude can help you to find inner peace because you're able to appreciate what you have in any given moment. When you're in a state of gratitude, you are not thinking of what you lack, and there's no comparison; there is only what is.

If you have not practised gratitude or want to strengthen your practice, begin by looking around you. What are you grateful for in this given moment? Are you grateful for being outside, sitting in a café, or having a roof over your head? Consider how you feel spirituality, mentally, and physically. We often get caught up in looking at the future and feeling dissatisfied with the present moment, but when you begin to turn inward and reflect on the present, you can experience gratitude. When you begin to appreciate what you have rather than dwelling on what you perceive to be missing, you can find joy, calm, and peace.

To begin, each morning or evening write down or say out loud three things you are grateful for. You may want to share this practice with your loved one, friends, or family. Not only does this help to keep you accountable to this practice but it also allows you to learn about what your loved ones are grateful for. Jesse and I share our 'three things' each night before we go to sleep. For us, it's a nice way to end the day and we go to sleep feeling a little calmer and in a more positive frame of mind.

I also find that practising gratitude while you are travelling is a powerful way to focus on each moment. You begin to centre yourself in the present and treasure the time rather than getting the holiday blues because you know that your time away is coming to an end.

In 2019, I decided to add to my gratitude practice by creating an achievements jar. I maintained my daily gratitude practice, but the achievements jar was a way of reminding myself of what I had achieved throughout the year. When I tried something new, achieved a goal, or started a project or a new job, I wrote down the date and a short description of what I had achieved. At the end of the year, I read the notes and it helped me to remember what I had accomplished during the year. On days when I felt like I wasn't making progress, I looked in my jar and it calmed me down. It helped me to get out of my own head. I moved from feeling frustrated to being grateful for what I had achieved, and I could see clearly that I was making progress.

If writing down three things you're grateful for or having an achievements jar doesn't resonate with you, that's okay. Try to think of other ways that you can practise gratitude each day. The most important part is to start. Once you begin to train your brain to search for the positive in a situation or day, you notice different parts of the environment you're in. You aren't limited to being grateful for what you have *right now*; you can also be grateful for what is yet to come. For instance, you may want to be grateful for what you will achieve in the future, such as getting your dream job, finding a fun hobby, falling in love, and so on. You can picture yourself in that moment, think of how you're feeling, and believe it has happened.

We all have challenging days, but it's on these days that having a gratitude practice will help you. Even if it's something small like getting fresh air, wearing an outfit that makes you feel confident, or a well-made coffee from your favourite coffee shop, you're still acknowledging that even though the day was difficult, there were still good parts. No day is filled with entirely bad moments. On these days, you look for the silver lining—your moments of gratitude. For instance, if you're focusing on it being a freezing cold morning then chances are you will miss the beauty of the sunrise because your mind is focused on something else in that moment. However, if you are open to being grateful, you can take a moment to notice the beauty of the sunrise and appreciate that you were able to see it.

Our perspective and mindset impacts how we respond to situations. All of us will experience the same situation differently and part of that is to do with our mindset. You can search for the negative or the positive in a situation, the choice is yours.

Ask yourself:

1. What does gratitude mean to you?
2. When were you last grateful for a moment or person or what you have?
3. What are five things that you are grateful for?
4. Take time to reach out to a loved one and tell them why you're grateful to have them in your life.
5. For twenty-one days, write down three things you are grateful for and see how you feel at the end.

Chapter 31

LESS FEAR, MORE GRATITUDE

Never let the fear of striking out keep you from the playing the game.
—BABE RUTH

Fear and love cannot be felt simultaneously. These two emotions are not roommates. When you feel fear, be curious and explore the feeling. Ask yourself what are you afraid of? What is the worst thing that can happen and what is the likelihood of it occurring?

When fear rules your mind, you become paralysed and play it safe. Rather than stepping into your growth zone, you retreat back into the familiar. Rather than being fearful of an opportunity, be grateful. It's a chance to learn something new and to better yourself. If you're afraid to fail, think of it as a learning opportunity. Remember, failing doesn't make you a failure.

By focusing on what you are a grateful for, you begin to change your mindset and the lens through which you are viewing the situation. Say your boss asks you to step up into a different role: you can either allow fear to take over and say no or you can feel the fear and say yes anyway. If you feel fear, try not to let it control your decisions. Instead, acknowledge it and be grateful for the opportunity and say yes.

Fear shows up in different ways in our lives. There's the fear that holds us back due to self-doubt, or the fear of the unknown, and then there's fear for your safety. One can save your life and the other can limit your potential. In relation to the fear that holds you back, consider whether you'd rather stay in your comfort zone or grow.

You can feel fear but still try anyway. Gratitude is not the absence of fear, rather it is the ability to move past your fear and step out of your comfort zone. It's about changing the way you are looking at the situation. Instead of thinking of the what-ifs, you instead can find a way to be grateful for the opportunity. If the situation didn't go to plan, you can learn from it. Once you start overcoming your fears, you can see what you're capable of. You now have an answer to the what-if and you have gained more knowledge in the process.

Be grateful that you were able to acknowledge the feeling and then try to feel the fear and do it anyway. When you know who you are and what you stand for, you will be okay. When an opportunity arises, it can be daunting because it can mean something new and unknown. It is in these moments we have a choice. We can either stand still or venture forward. Face the fear or let it rule us. You can choose to be grateful or you can be fearful of the opportunity.

Either way, you have made a choice. If you acknowledge the fear, face it, and proceed, then you are empowering yourself. When you step into your growth zone, the outcome is unknown, but if you retreat back into your comfort zone, then there will be no change.

If fear creeps in, say 'hello' and write down your fears or worries. The less power you give fear, the stronger you will become. Fear is a glass ceiling that we place over our own heads. We listen to our self-limiting beliefs rather than trying and letting an opportunity unfold. Sometimes the only person standing between you and your goal is yourself. Instead, we settle for comfort, retreat to our safe zones, and then ask the what-if questions. If you face fear, then you will know the answer—no what-if needed.

You either succeed or you learn. Either way, you grow. Try not to settle for comfort; you won't be able to grow in this space. Settle for continual growth and movement as opposed to standing still. Be grateful for opportunities when they're presented to you. If you decline an opportunity, ask yourself why. Is it due to fear? If it is, then apply the above principles, get curious, and re-evaluate your decision.

We are all novices until we learn more. A master wasn't always one. Knowledge must be learned to be had. When we live our lives in a state of gratitude rather than a state of fear, things flow easier. You can move with grace and see abundance rather than lack. You can accept opportunities and learn from mistakes rather than never trying at all.

Chapter 32

SELF-FULL

Earlier in the book, I briefly mentioned how the language we use matters. So, let's just clear something up: looking after yourself is *not* selfish—it's self-full. I don't normally have big 'a-ha' moments, but when it came to this topic, I did.

A little while I ago, I decided to purchase an expensive but insanely delicious-smelling candle made by a local business. As I was paying for it, the cashier asked if it was a gift for someone to which I said no. Without thinking, I said it was something for me and it was selfish to which the cashier replied with, 'It's not selfish, it's self-full.'

When I arrived home that afternoon, I took some time to reflect on what the cashier said. I don't know why I thought that purchasing an expensive candle for myself was selfish, especially when I have a full-time job, pay the bills on time, make donations, and happen to have some leftover money most weeks. Why would it be selfish of me to make a mindful purchase to buy something that would bring me joy? I adored the scent and knew it would be a candle that I would use when I was having a bath to create a relaxing and soothing space.

The cashier unknowingly gave me permission to look at my self-purchased gift in a different light. I felt content. It was a revelation. I made a choice to spend my money on something which would enrich my life. Furthermore, her comment uplifted me as it's a reminder that we need to take care of ourselves and it is not selfish to give yourself a gift.

If we want to give our best to the world, then we need to fill our cups up first. We can only go so far or do so much before we need to recharge. It is not selfish to take care of yourself, it is self-full.

Instead, we ignore our body's warning signs (such as fatigue, hunger, or illness) and go beyond our limits. We are all human and we need time to rest. We were not built to run for days on end without sleep. I mean, you can try to pull an all-nighter or two in a row and let me know how that goes. I doubt you'll be feeling great or functioning at your optimum level. When life gets full, we cut out things that we don't see as a priority, and for many, one of those things is self-care. It's a pity that self-care routines are typically the first thing to be removed because it is during these times when self-care is of utmost importance. You need to give yourself a chance to recover. Be self-full as much as you can. You can start with once a week, then twice, and so on. Notice the change when you bring it back into your routine.

I think many of us have experienced the feelings caused when you are hangry or been around someone who has reached that state and know that it's not pretty. We know we can perform better, and once we have had food, we feel more like ourselves. It is highly unlikely that you will perform at your best when you are exhausted, which is why it is so important to be self-full. When we reach the stages of burnout, we become like our hangry selves. If you want to bring your A-game to the world each day, it starts with a solid self-care routine.

Otherwise, when we are exhausted our tolerance threshold decreases significantly, minor issues become major causes of frustration, and our ability to solve complex problems or think with clarity or creativity also becomes impaired.

Living in a state of fatigue is detrimental to ourselves and those around us. We are not able to perform at our best, we can hurt others with our words and actions, plus the likelihood of making errors that you wouldn't make otherwise also increases. In addition to these factors, it can also reduce your lifespan. When you have a gift to offer the world, the more time you have to share it, the better. So, start to consider some self-full ways you can look after yourself.

Having a non-negotiable self-care routine is crucial as it will become one of your cornerstones. It will enable you to give your best, be your best, and perform at your best. It isn't easy to create a routine as with any new habit you are wanting to incorporate into your life, adjustments will need to be made, but after a few days or weeks, you will begin to notice the difference. It's like when you break free from your everyday routine and suddenly the everyday stresses fade away and you remember what it's like to not feel so stressed. The same will happen when you begin to look after you. You are your best friend, for better or for worse. You will always be there for you. So, treat yourself with the love, care, and kindness you deserve. Be self-full—it isn't selfish.

Chapter 33

SELF-CARE

What words or images come to mind when you think of self-care? Is it a luxury retreat, a cabin in the mountains, whole foods, fashionable outfits, spa days, or having an in-house sanctuary with white walls, fresh linen, and a tonne of cushions on a sofa?

In recent years, self-care has become somewhat of a buzzword. *Oxford Dictionary* defines self-care as the 'practice of taking action to preserve or improve one's health'. It also defines it as the 'practice of taking an active role in protecting one's own well-being and happiness, in particular during periods of stress.'

Based on the dictionary definition, we can see that self-care is a practice. It's a personal practice which focuses on doing things that make *you* feel good. If you haven't created a self-care practice before, or yours has fallen by the wayside, I'd suggest allocating time this week to one thing that makes you feel good. There are so many options out there and it's not about what looks good or sounds good to others, it's completely about you. If the thought of sitting in a bathtub with bubbles and a candle doesn't light you up, don't do it. Self-care is all about finding things that we can add into our daily routines to take care of ourselves. It's not for the socials or others; this is something especially for you.

I hinted at it above, but I truly believe that self-care is a highly personalised practice. You may need to try a few things before you find what works for you. It's not a one-size-fits-all approach, and an activity which may make someone else feel amazing may not give you the same result. Some may consider meditation or yoga as a form of self-care while others would prefer to go for a run or swim. Instead of comparing your practice to someone else, find one that feels right for you. Learn to tune in to your body and listen to what it needs. Some mornings I will wake up and all I want to do is a short yoga practice while other mornings it may be a guided meditation and other mornings, nothing at all. It isn't laziness or a lack of willpower, I am simply allowing myself to listen to what I need for that day.

Typically, when life gets full, self-care is omitted from our schedules to make time for other tasks. It is imperative, especially during stressful, busy, and emotional times that we schedule time for ourselves. Make time for a self-care practice even if it's only five or ten minutes. This will help you to recharge, reduce your stress levels, and limit the chance of becoming burnt out and emotionally spent. You deserve to take care of yourself.

It may seem convenient to omit the practice, however the short and long term implications are not worth it. We cannot be outwardly productive every minute of the day. We need time to be inwardly productive, to recharge and unwind. Just as you can function on minimal sleep for a period of time, you can neglect your self-care practice, but it comes at a price. When your self-care routine is absent from your life, you may start to become unsettled, frustrated, and resentful. You are in control of how you spend your time so ensure that you allocate time to take care of you.

In general, I believe that women especially (sorry guys) may feel guilty or consider a self-care practice to be selfish, but it is not. Self-care is not selfish, so please challenge your own beliefs and the false truths you may be telling yourself. If we want to perform at our best, feel like ourselves, have vitality and be present, we need to give ourselves the opportunity to do so and that starts with self-care.

A self-care practice gives you a chance to focus on yourself, check in with how you are feeling, and look inward. It gives you space to do something which brings you joy, helps to ground you, and clear your mind. It is a chance to reduce the white noise and be with yourself.

Your self-care practice may incorporate something for your mind, body, and/or soul. What activities make you feel good? Some examples include:

- Massage.
- Having a bubble bath.
- Baking/cooking.
- Yoga.
- Dancing.

- Reading.
- Listening to a podcast.
- Workout.
- Nature walk.
- Swimming.
- Focusing on your breath.
- Journal.
- Creative hobby.
- Gardening.
- Meditation.
- Road trip/staycation by yourself.

Ask yourself:

1. How do you define self-care?
2. Do you have a daily ritual?
3. If so, does it help you to feel recharged?
4. If not, what is a new practice you can try?
5. Do you consider self-care to be a necessity or luxury and why?

Chapter 34

VISION BOARDS—A WAY TO CREATE

Manifestation has multiple facets. For the purpose of this chapter, I'll define 'manifesting' as making something clear or obvious to the eye or mind. By creating a vision board, you are giving yourself a visual prompt to help you make your goals clearer and hopefully bring them to life. You can write and repeat mantras, meditate, or visualise what you want to welcome into your life. Creating a vision board enables you to think about what you want to welcome into your life and it can serve as a daily visual reminder of what you are working towards.

I have had a vision board for a few years, and at the beginning of each year I take time to make changes to my board. I mainly use pictures and quotes on my board; each of which is tied to a goal. I have images related to my short-term, medium-term, and long-term goals in different areas of my life. For example, with my upcoming wedding, I have photos of couples dancing and of a father walking his daughter down the aisle. It allows me to visualise our first dance and how it will feel having my dad walk me down the aisle when the day comes. A longer-term goal is to move into a larger home in a different suburb. I have photos up on my board of two-storey houses, interiors, and backyards to reflect this.

Pictures paint a thousand words, so make it count. Vision boards are personal, and it can be easy to fall into the trap of creating a board which appeals to others. If it doesn't motivate you, speak to you, or inspire you to achieve your goals, it's not going to work—full stop. If you put images on your vision board which represent a life that you don't want to lead (such as owning luxury cars, a fancy home, or the latest piece of technology) then it's a waste of time. It's blunt but true. There's no point in curating a board which doesn't align with your values or life's vision. Focus on what will bring you joy, the life *you* want to lead. Get creative and find images, quotes, and so forth that resonate with you.

A vision board can help bring your dreams and goals to life through pictures and quotes. It can help you visualise your goals and the moment when you'll achieve them. When your board represents your *why* and your short-, medium-, and long-term goals, it can inspire you to continue on your journey. It serves as a reminder of what you are working towards and if (or when) you get sidetracked, it can help you regain focus. You can look at your board and know exactly what you're working towards.

When we have goals to work towards, it gives us focus. For instance, if you say you will save money but don't have a specific reason in mind, it is harder to save money. Sure, it makes sense to have money set aside for an emergency, but if your goals are not specific, you will find it challenging to achieve them. Being specific with your goals gives you clarity, and when you're tempted to deviate, your *why* will be so compelling that it will keep you in check. You need a *why*, an underlying reason that is driving you.

Before curating your own vision board, you may want to consider what goals you want your board to represent. Are you wanting to travel, buy your own house, start up a business, get married, buy a car, renovate your house, write a book, start a side project, get a pet, or meet an idol? These are just a few ideas.

Your vision board is a representation of you and what you'd like your future life/self to look like. Once you've worked out what goals you want to focus on, the next step is to find the materials to create the board. Op shops are a great way to source magazines, or you can even go to local swap meets, post a wanted ad online, or print images directly from the internet. If there's a place or person you'd like to meet, why not get creative and photoshop a photo of you with the person or in the location? The more visual you can make the board the better.

Chapter 35

THE POWER OF JOURNALLING

Journalling is a way of putting pen to paper to write down what happened each day or for you to write down what is on your mind. You can tap into your subconscious and let the words flow without judgement. It can be a used as a record keeping activity (that is, keeping a daily journal), or it can be therapeutic or creative.

Journalling offers many benefits including improving memory function and calming your mind; it offers a space for reflection, can boost your mood by allowing you to work through your feelings rather than supressing them, and provides you with a way to track your goals. Lastly, it can spark creativity because you are giving yourself a space to sit with your thoughts without judgement.

Over the years, I have changed the way that I use my journal. While I still maintain a journal for each day of the year, I try to focus on my thoughts and feelings as well as three things (at minimum) that I was grateful for that day. In the past, I used to document each thing I did during that day, like a recollection of events, and I'd include song lyrics to a song that I had stuck in my head that day. In addition to my daily journal, I have one that I write my weekly goals in. I also track my daily habits and write down my to do list as well.

I know others who use journals as a creative outlet to create sketches, free write, or create pieces of artwork. There is no one way to keep a journal; it's just about finding a way that resonates with you.

If you haven't written a journal before, or the thought of it just absolutely doesn't appeal to you, keep in mind that you don't have to write yourself a 'Dear diary' entry each day, nor do you have to write an essay. It's completely up to you if it's something that you want to try and you can always try by writing a sentence each day that kind of wraps up or sums up your day. Journalling is a practice that can be done daily or less often depending on how you want to journal. It should be an outlet rather than a chore so if you feel like it may be too much to try to implement it into your life on a daily basis, aim for once a week or fortnight.

You can be positive and negative; it can be a short sentence or a long sentence. It's up to you to determine what journalling looks like for you. There is no right or wrong approach. It's a personal activity and not one standard way suits every person.

You can always begin by using a journal to record any appointments. If you have a busy workload, you can always begin with a work journal. Once you get into the habit of writing in your work journal, you can then begin a personal journal. I would suggest keeping two journals: one for work, and one for personal use just so they don't get mixed up. You could then leave your work one at work and keep another journal on you.

I use journalling as an outlet, a way of recording my days, thoughts, and feelings. It also gives me something to look back on if I want to reflect on the past. On days when I'm feeling a little down, I'll often go through a journal to remind myself what I have achieved.

Alternatively, if you meditate, you could keep a journal near you. This gives you the option to write down any thoughts or feelings you had during your meditation. You can simply let your pen be guided by your thoughts. Your words may not even be your own.

Chapter 36

TREATS AND REWARDS— WHAT'S THE DIFFERENCE?

Treats and rewards may sound similar but in actuality, they are two different things. A *treat* is something to have in moderation. It is not attached to a goal or achievement, and it is something you allow yourself to have—just because. *Rewards* are result-based and are often tied to an outcome, goal, or achievement. Once you have accomplished what you intended to, you then allow yourself to reap the reward.

Rewards are earned. If you want some additional motivation for achieving a goal, why not determine the reward you will give yourself once it has been completed? That way you get the satisfaction of having completed a goal and get a tangible reward for doing so. This can be great to do at the goal-setting stage. When you're writing down your goal, determine what your reward will be. For the outset, it doesn't always need to be a physical reward such as a meal out, a new outfit, or an experience. It could instead be an intrinsic reward such as a sense of accomplishment or personal growth. Think of the reward as an intangible thing such as a thought or feeling. Visualise yourself achieving the goal and the feelings and emotions it brings up for you and write that down as your reward.

As an example, when I complete a home workout, I don't reward myself with a snack afterwards. Instead, my reward is a feeling of satisfaction and, to be frank, sore muscles (if it's a strength workout). Rewards can be beneficial in helping you achieve your goal because you know that there's something waiting for you at the finish line. It allows you to dig into your energy reserves when you're feeling low on willpower and you can push through because, let's face it, there are some days when we simply aren't feeling it.

If you're looking at implementing a rewards system, it's important to set some ground rules. Decide when you will give yourself a reward and what the purpose of the reward is. The reward should be received after you have achieved the goal rather than beforehand. It's there to celebrate your achievement rather than bribe you to do something. The aim is delayed gratification rather than instant gratification.

I'd recommend rewarding yourself for achieving a goal rather than when you're trying to form a habit. Think of it this way: if you reward yourself each day that you're building a habit and then once it's become a habit you remove the reward, how likely are you to continue? Let's use the gym as an example. If you reward yourself with something each time you do a workout and take said reward away when it's become a habit, you may find it difficult to keep up the habit. When you link a reward to a habit, you are subconsciously telling yourself that the only reason you are doing that task is because of the reward, and when the reward goes away you will no longer have the motivation to continue on with the habit. Attach a reward to the attainment of a goal rather than celebrating that you have begun to form a habit.

In addition to this, it's important to decide what type of rewards you want to have. If you value eating whole foods, then rewarding yourself with greasy takeout wouldn't support your values. It may be beneficial to steer clear of food rewards as it can be detrimental rather than beneficial. If you implement an unhealthy reward or one that doesn't align with your values, it creates a conflict. Align your rewards with your habits and lifestyle rather than creating conflict. What one person considers a reward may not appeal to you. Think of what motivates you both intrinsically and materialistically when curating your rewards list.

Some of the things on my rewards list include intrinsic satisfaction, a celebratory meal, going on a road trip or nature walk, a beach walk, having a nap, attending a workshop, reading a book or purchasing a new book, having a barista-made coffee, or going to an event.

Let's move on to treats. If food comes to mind as soon as you hear the word treats, I'm with you there. In the context of this chapter, treats are more than just a food item. Unlike rewards, treats aren't linked to the achievement of your goals. A treat is something you allow yourself to indulge in 'just because'. You may treat yourself to a glass of wine at the end of the week or have a monthly massage. There is no ulterior motive with a treat: regardless of what you do or don't do, you get the treat. You don't have to justify it to yourself.

Just like rewards, the same principles apply when you're curating your treats list. While this may not be true for all of us, typically when we think of treats, we think of cheat meals or unhealthy food items. If you choose to treat yourself to a food item, be mindful and listen to your body. A treat should be pleasurable rather than inflicting feelings of guilt and shame.

While it may seem okay to give yourself a food-based reward which provides a few moments of pleasure, it is imperative that you consider the aftermath. Typically, if we have a treat, then our negative self-talk takes over and we feel guilt. So, what I would suggest is that—instead of self-sabotaging treats—you write a list of things that inspire you or bring you joy. Then you can choose from that list when you feel like a treat. These treats can uplift you rather than inflict feelings of guilt and shame that can come from misaligned treats.

Below is an example of some of my go-to treats.

- Massage or spa treatment.
- Barista-made coffee.
- Staycation.
- Clothing.
- Buying a new book.
- Having a bath.
- Reading a book.

- Staying at home.
- Sleeping in.
- Watching a movie.

Ask yourself:

1. How do I define treats?
2. What are some feel good treats?
3. Are these treats serving me well?
4. How do I define rewards?
5. What are some feel good rewards?
6. Are these rewards serving me well?

Chapter 37

TRY SOMETHING NEW

Life is either a daring adventure or nothing.
—HELEN KELLER

The above is a quote I read many years ago and it has stuck with me ever since. It serves as a reminder than we can choose to live a rich and meaningful life, or we can choose to live a life with little adventure. Now, adventure doesn't necessarily mean boarding a plane and travelling somewhere; it relates to your interaction with the world. Are you willing to try new things and learn something new or would you prefer to stay within a stable routine where much of it is the same? In order to thrive, I believe that we need some certainty, but we also need an element of uncertainty to keep our body, mind, and soul stimulated.

Routine, habits, and rituals can be grounding but they can also make us complacent. If you stick to what you know, you won't grow. When we take risks or try something new, we are venturing out of our comfort zone momentarily. This can be daunting if you prefer to feel like you're in control. However, the longer you reside solely in your

159

comfort zone, the more fear you may feel when you decide to venture out of it—if you do at all. Acknowledge the fear and push through. Growth resides on the other side of your comfort zone. That's where the magic happens.

When we find ourselves in a rut, our behaviours have become automated. Life becomes monotonous because you are doing the same things day in and day out. Considering that our conscious mind comprises only 5% of our brain,[14] the fewer behaviours we have that are automated, the better. After we reach thirty, many of our behaviours become automated, so if you stick to routine and what you know, then you will run on autopilot more often than not. If we don't welcome novelty and newness into our lives, we become fixed. Life continues to move around us, but we are set in stone. Would you rather be moving forward or remain where you are?

Living life solely in your comfort zone doesn't make you immune from the seasons of life. If we allow fear to rule our minds, sticking just to what we know, we miss out on opportunities, growth, experience, and learning. Mistakes are not final. If we live in fear, too afraid to try something new for fear it may not work out or we might make a mistake, we will miss out on opportunities, growing, and learning. Things don't always have to work out the way you envision them to. It's a part of life, and there's beauty in the unknown.

Let's use love as an example. Many of us have experienced heartbreak or rejection. You take a chance on a relationship only for it to not work out. You have two options when this happens: to not try again or to heal and move forward. Sometimes, the disasters or unexpected outcomes make for a good story later on. There's often a lesson to be discovered in the situation, and while you may not see it at first, it will show itself. The same applies to broader aspects of life. Trust in your abilities, be courageous, and see trying new things as a way to learn more about yourself. You live and learn. Experiences give you knowledge and if you fail, you can try again. Experience is an essential part of life and the more experiences we acquire, the richer our life will be.

Remind yourself that you are showing courage by stepping out of your comfort zone. Along the way, you may discover an untapped passion or interest in a subject. When I was younger, I wasn't interested in baking. When I'm cooking, I like to add in ingredients or change the recipe slightly, and to bake well you need to be okay with precise measurements and following the method accurately. When I did start to bake, I realised how much I enjoyed the process and measuring out the ingredients wasn't so bad after all. I also learned that once you get the base recipe figured out, you can add in extra ingredients. My go-to baking recipe is banana bread, and while the base ingredients remain the same, I always add in something extra to make it different. Now, I'd consider baking a hobby of mine. We can either allow our perceptions of an activity to limit ourselves or we can challenge ourselves by trying something new. Not all perceptions or assumptions are correct.

If you try something new and it doesn't work out, that's okay. It doesn't mean you are a failure. You have stepped out of your comfort zone and tried something new which is courageous. Trying something new doesn't necessarily mean to become an extreme sports fanatic unless that's what you want to do. It could be trying a new recipe, going to an event you wouldn't normally consider, styling your hair differently, watching a movie you wouldn't normally, or trying a new workout. All of these things get you out of your comfort zone in a less extreme way. If you start with small steps, you build confidence and from there you can do something bigger.

If you have trouble thinking about what you might want to do, you can always picture yourself at the end of your life and reflect on what you have done. What would you want to experience before it's over? Novelty makes life exciting, and while our brains like routine, they also crave novelty.

Create a 'bucket list' and try to schedule time to tick items off occasionally. Instead of asking for a gift for your birthday, you could always ask for money towards an experience or the experience itself. Personally, I use my birthday as a reason to do something different, whether it be a road trip away, a meal at a new restaurant, or an experience. I find that it's enough to break the routine and a yearly reminder to myself to be adventurous and do something new. It's also the reason why I enjoy travelling as much as I do. Travel encourages you to step out of your comfort zone and immerse yourself in a new culture or place.

Where I can, I give the gift of experiences to Jesse, friends, and family. As adults, we typically are able to buy ourselves the things we want, and yet the items on the bucket list remain un-ticked. So, instead of being the giver of objects, I choose to be the giver of experiences. Not only does it make the birthday recipient happy, but it also brings you joy as you are able to give a meaningful gift.

We only get one life, so why not try new things, take a chance, and see where it leads. Knowing is better than a what-if.

Ask yourself:

1. Write down a bucket list and pick one to do in the next three months.
2. Record the date you ticked it off the list and how you felt before and after you did it.
3. When was the last time you did something new?
4. What activities do you want to try?
5. Encourage your family, love, or friends to create their own list.

Chapter 38

BE PRESENT BY LIVING IN THE MOMENT

Choose your phone or the person sitting opposite you.
You cannot give both your full attention.

When you live in the past or future, you miss today. I like to think of it as living life on replay or fast forward. You're physically present, but mentally you are somewhere else. When you are not fully present, you may regret not taking in the moment as it unfolded later on.

Technology enables us to capture moments on a device that can be replayed at a later time. The trade-off for this means that you are not fully present when the moment actually happens. You're worried about missing the moment, so you snapshot it instead. When you replay the video or look back on the photos, can you remember the moment vividly or is it just a blur?

Take concerts as an example. A lot of people will be on their phones or have a camera out when the artist is on stage. Rather than being completely immersed in the moment, they're recording a song or taking photos. I used to spend a lot of time at concerts doing this exact thing, and then I realised I was missing out on the moment. I didn't get to completely experience the concert because I was trying to record and take photos that I thought would look nice. I also realised that I was taking photos for others, either to show off (thanks, ego) or to share a recording to explain how good I thought the performance was. I rarely looked back at the photos or recordings after that. I urge you to consider who are you taking the photos and recordings for. Is it for you or is it for others? Even when we're told that photos and recordings aren't permitted, there is still someone that cannot control their urge to break the rule. Having a 'no recordings' rule gives us an opportunity to actually be present and focus our attention on the artist. Isn't that what we pay the money for in the first place? Once I limited the amount of time I spent on my phone at concerts, I discovered that I was more present and the memory I have of that event is much clearer. I remember how I felt, the energy in the room, and the songs sung. If you take photos and recordings out of fear that you'll forget, you won't.

As the saying goes, stop and smell the roses. Be in the moment rather than allowing it to pass you by. We spend our lives waiting for the big moments, and yet when they arrive, we sometimes don't experience it completely. Let's use getting engaged as an example. I was hopeful that one day a guy would be willing to get on one knee and ask me to marry him. When Jesse popped the question, I was half-listening to what he was saying because I was nervous once I worked out that he was trying to propose. Fortunately, I stopped trying to point out the snow-topped mountains, faced him, and let myself be present in the moment. All I saw was Jesse. I wasn't thinking of anything else; I was simply listening to what he was asking me. A year on, I still remember this moment vividly.

A few years earlier, I saw snow for the first time. One of my most treasured photos is one of me standing in the middle of a road with the snow falling down around me. While it's nice to have the photo, the image in my mind is still very vivid. I remember the feelings—a mixture of joy and excitement as well as the colours. If I didn't fully experience that moment, my recollection of that day wouldn't be the same.

Let's be clear: I am not always fully present. There have been many occasions where I have not been as present as I wish I had been. At my engagement party, I was helping to hand out the appetisers, greet guests, and ensuring that it was running smoothly. At the end of the event I was exhausted, and to be honest, it didn't really feel like a party had just happened. I played host rather than allowing myself to mingle and celebrate with everyone. If you find yourself wishing you were more present, learn from that experience and try to be more present moving forward. There more present we are, the more we can enjoy the moments of our lives as they unfold.

Often, we look to the future or to the past rather than being present. We tell ourselves that in the future we'll be happier, healthier, have a new job, have more money in the bank, and so forth. Happiness can be found in the now. In the present, there is no worrying about the future or regret for the past, there is merely one moment unfolding ever so beautifully.

When you're distracted by thoughts, technology, or trying to multitask, you cannot be fully present. As a quick example of how technology hinders our ability to be focused in the moment, there have been times when I've been on my phone and Jesse has tried to tell me something and I haven't heard a word he said. It's not that I was trying to be rude or ignore him, I just couldn't give him my full attention while I was on my phone. In relation to your life as a whole, it can result in a life that has not been fully appreciated as you have simply rushed from one moment to another without revelling in the present. Give your presence to the present and you will be rewarded with beautiful memories.

While it is only natural to look forward to the future, there are three things to be mindful of:

1. Saying that you *will be … in the future*, without focusing on how you can make that a reality.
2. Living in the future most of the time.
3. Being dissatisfied with your current circumstances; striving only for perceived future happiness by missing out on what is happening now.

Let's discuss the first point in more detail. If you spend your days living in the future, then you may find you are missing out on your life as it's unfolding. You'll miss the small moments which may become a regret in your later life. It's normal to be excited about an upcoming event, holiday, or activity. While anticipation is great and I am someone who counts down the days until a holiday, if this is your sole focus, you miss out on being present. The little things are the big things. Whether it be taking in the moment when you first say 'I love you' to your partner, the first kiss, the proposal, your first day at your dream job, buying a house, time with your family, celebrating a special occasion, getting married, moments with your children, and so forth. Try to be as present as you can be. Once that moment has passed, it's gone for good.

When I was a child, I dreamt of nothing more than to be an adult. I wanted to listen to the grown-ups' conversations and be treated like an adult. Much to my dismay, I had a lot of growing up to do and was often told that the adults were having a conversation. I'd sometimes say that I couldn't wait to be an adult and my parents would say something along the lines of 'enjoy being a kid, you have the rest of your life to be an adult.' When we are looking forward to the next chapter of our lives, we miss the present. You will never be as young as you are right now so make the most of it. As children, especially, we cannot wait to be grown up and we miss part of the fun of being a child in the process. Then as adults, many of us yearn for the simplicity of childhood.

The simple act of waking up and living for another day is something which we often take for granted, but it is our greatest gift. We are given the opportunity to live another day. It's another day that we can do something which brings us joy, remind loved ones how much we value them, and be grateful for who we are and what we have. We expect that we will be here tomorrow, but ultimately, one day will be our last. So, where you can, take a moment to be grateful for another day.

Our days turn into weeks, which turn into months, and the months turn into the years which makes up the chapters of our lives. Each day we have the chance to write a new verse or stick to the same chorus. The choice is yours. You're the composer of your life's work. Your past does not need to determine your future. It's unwritten; it's yours to shape how you please. You can allow the past situations, attitudes, and habits to guide you into the future or you can make the choice to change today. You can begin to change your habits and create a new future for yourself in this present moment.

When we are present, we can appreciate where we are on our journey rather than focusing solely on the destination which will arrive in its own time. If you want to live a more meaningful life, take time to appreciate moments. Challenge yourself to focus on a single task rather than multitask. If you're going for walk, leave your phone at home and notice your surroundings. Use your senses to become present: what can you see, hear, or feel? Sometimes we focus on the destination and miss the journey. It's as though our brains go into autopilot and we space out. By learning to be more present, you can be more conscious.

Whether you're literally or metaphorically climbing a mountain, your main focus on the journey is reaching the top. When you reach the summit, the view is spectacular, but it's the endurance, grit, and resilience you showed to get there that matters. Other times, you may achieve a goal and think to yourself, *Is that it*? Or you may acknowledge the achievement briefly before moving on to the next thing. Allow yourself to celebrate what you have achieved—both the journey and the destination.

Your journey matters. It is where your stories, growth, and learning comes from. The destination is just the result of the steps you have taken to get there. There are times when you may want to retreat, the terrain seems too treacherous, or you've reached a level of exhaustion, but in those moments you have two choices: to push through the pain and get the second dose of energy or you can turn around and walk back down. It is in the present moment that you can create your future.

You can either walk through life like a zombie, merely existing and not taking in the moments, or you can be present and allow yourself to immerse yourself in your surroundings to take in the good, the messy, and the ugly moments knowing that it is all of these moments which create your life. Choose to be present and take it all in one moment at a time.

Chapter 39

A FULL LIFE VERSUS A BUSY LIFE

When you change your thoughts and language used, you begin to change how you live your life. If you wake up in the morning thinking about how busy you are going to be, this often results in feeling stressed. Your brain begins to run through all the tasks you want/feel obligated to accomplish that day. Chances are you will feel frazzled from the moment you wake up.

It doesn't need to be this way. Instead, you can begin your days with a moment of gratitude. Think about how *full* rather than *busy* your day is and over time, you will begin to notice a shift in your perspective and mood. For many of us, *busy* is a word which holds a negative connotation while *full* represents abundance and choice.

Busy often means keeping yourself occupied or having a lot to do. Busyness can imply that you are stressed, frazzled, or rushing from one thing to the next. In contrast, *full* means having no empty space and not lacking anything. Fullness can imply richness and abundance.

The language we use to communicate with others and our internal dialogue matters. It has an impact on our mindset, mood, and actions. Take a moment to write down the words you associate with the term 'busy' including any emotional responses you have. Once you have recorded your responses, do the same word association activity for the word 'full'. Once you have completed the activity, compare the words you associate with *full* and *busy* and see if there are any similarities and differences. Notice how each word makes you feel on a physical level. Does one word cause you to feel tense and another relaxed? Do you feel stressed or calm?

Personally, the word *busy* has a negative energy attached to it. If I tell myself or others that I have a busy day ahead, I feel stressed and tense in my shoulders. I feel as though the day has gotten away from me and that I am no longer in control to the degree I would like. The word *full* has a more positive and calming energy attached to it. If I tell myself that I have a full day, I feel like I am in control of how I am spending my time. I feel calmer and more excited about the day ahead. By reflecting on how each word makes me feel, I have made a conscious effort to refrain from using the word *busy* as much as I used to and replaced it with the word *full* because I feel better when I say my days are full rather than busy.

It is these seemingly small changes which have a great impact on your life. A full life is one that is not rushed, it is filled with chosen moments and allows you to be present and grateful for each day, while a busy life may be filled with many tasks, be fast-paced, and passes by quickly. You tend to be more future-focused, thinking about the next task while you're in the middle of completing the current one. Slow down; life a full life rather than a busy one.

Chapter 40

DAILY HABITS SHAPE OUR LIVES

Step by step and the thing is done.
—CHARLES ATLAS

What we do each day matters. Daily actions shape our days, weeks, months, and years. Over time, our daily habits add up, like compound interest. You may not notice any changes at first (such as overindulging in food and not exercising) but over time, it leads to weight gain. And vice versa: if you work out daily, you may not see any changes to your physique but over time, you build muscle and become fitter and leaner.

It can be tempting to put off an actionable task for a tomorrow that never comes, but if you show grit and keep focused even on days when motivation eludes you, you can achieve success. If there is such a thing as a secret to success, it lies in your daily habits and routine. It's the seemingly invisible actions you do each day which enhance your life. Just as the little things mean the most when we reflect on moments shared with loved one, the same applies when looking at our habits.

Life goes by at a rapid pace, and yet many of us seem to live life on fast forward, going straight from task to task. We forget that things take time in a world where we need it done yesterday, so if we don't see results quickly, we move on to the next novel thing. Take, for instance, dieting. Fad or crash diets are attractive for those who want to see an instant result. They eliminate the need for hard work, and while they may work for some, the remainder see results with consistent daily actions over the long term instead. Rather than making a lifestyle change, we opt for the seemingly easier option such as a 21-day cleanse or detox, hoping that a short-term change will yield long-term success, but this is seldom the case. I am not intentionally trying to knock short programs as they can be beneficial. I am merely suggesting that habits are the same: if you do something a small amount of the time, it may have a small impact, but the impact would be greater if it were something you did most or every day.

We romanticise the notion of being an instant success. If we don't see a result from our work in a short time frame, we call it a failure and move on. This is where patience and grit helps. Just because it hasn't happened immediately doesn't mean it won't. Change takes time to produce noticeable effects. Once you accept that, progress happens. Focus on the input rather than a desired outcome.

Remind yourself that the notion of being an overnight success is a myth. Individuals who have achieved and sustained success in their chosen fields have gained it over time. We may only see the finished product, and if it reaches the mass market soon or goes viral, we believe it happened instantly, but all we are seeing is the finished product rather than what has gone into it. Some 'overnight' successes are years in the making.

If you are wanting to build lasting habits which will help you shape the life you want to lead, be realistic about the time it will take. Gratification will likely not be instant. Intent + actions = an outcome. Just as Rome was not built in a day, neither is the life we dream of. Imagine if we could achieve all of our dreams in a single day: what we would have left to look forward to?

To improve your patience, you should be prepared to change your mindset. Accept that things will take the time that they take and we cannot rush it. Mediate on it, create your own mantra, or show faith. As the saying goes, there is no elevator to success, only stairs. We cannot fast forward to our day of success, we simply have to put in the hard work and trust that the day will arrive. Life doesn't work according to our schedules. So, to create habits that will enable you to achieve your goals, your approach needs to change. If you try to rush what will be, then you get in your own way. Another way that you block yourself from opportunities or creating your dream life is if your habits do not serve you. Our habits shape our lives. If you want to get toned and build muscle, sitting on the couch and eating a tonne of processed foods isn't going to get you there. I wish we could think it into happening, but sadly, it hasn't worked for me yet.

It's time to let go of the idea of becoming an overnight success and instead focus on building your skills and cultivating daily habits that will enable you to improve and stay positive. We believe that if we aren't a natural, or after a week we see no results, it's time to move on to the next-best thing. We get in our own way when we don't give ourselves time. Instead, wait for your input to catch up to you and accept that any form of growth takes time.

If you're struggling to free yourself of this false truth, get reading or listening. There are many people who have achieved great success in their lives who are honest enough to explain how long their overnight successes took. Study the masters and take comfort in knowing that it takes the time that it takes.

Mastery takes time. Those who are at the top of their chosen field are often idolised and they deserve to be. Why? Because they have put in the time to become great. If you want to progress from novice to success, you have to start. Masters make it look simple. There's a high degree of skill and experience required to make a craft look simple. When you watch a musician perform, an artist paint, or athlete perform, they make it look effortless. That's not by chance, it's the result of being patient, investing time and practice. It's attainable, it's possible for you to reach that stage too.

You may have natural talent, and in the beginning it can be a great motivator, but if you believe that your natural talent will suffice, then you will likely be overtaken by those who have put in the hours to master their chosen field. Practice leads to mastery when one has the skills and capabilities to get there. Invest in yourself and give the task, goal, or habit adequate time. Be patient and monitor your progress. Trust the process.

Chapter 41

HABIT AUDITS AND HABIT SWITCHING

Out with the old, in with the new.

Charles Duhigg authored the book *The Power of Habit*.[15] It was one of the first books I had read on habits and it changed my perspective. I thought ingrained habits were near-impossible to change and that the only way to break a habit was to eliminate it. It turns out that there's more than one way to try to break a habit or introduce a new one into your life. So, let me introduce you to the idea of habit audits and habit switching.

Habit audits allow us to look at the habits we currently have while habit switching gives us a way to remove and install a new habit into our life simultaneously by switching one with the other. For instance, if you want to drink more tea and less coffee, you can perform a habit switch by replacing your coffee with tea. It doesn't leave an empty space where your old habit was; it creates space for the new one instead.

If our daily actions and habits shape our lives, are yours aligned with your goals and dreams? Chances are that not all the habits you currently have in your daily routines are serving you well. By doing an audit of your current habits, you can establish whether your habits are serving you well or if it's time to eliminate them from your life. Easy in theory but challenging in real life.

Let me give you an example. Jesse and I decided that to make dinnertime easier, we would sit down and write out a dinner plan for the following week. Easy. We stuck to this for a few months and then I let the habit slide. I didn't feel like eating what we had agreed to have for dinner, and shortly after the habit of having a dinner plan faded away. This habit was great because it meant I could cook meals in advance and not have to worry about thinking of what to have for dinner that night. It also meant Jesse could help put ideas forward.

Habits are deeply ingrained and some we do without any conscious thought because it has become automatic, such as a brushing your teeth. While you're doing your habit audit, try to think of the automatic habits you may have. Consider whether they are serving or hindering your progress. The purpose of this activity is to identify your habits, to consider whether they are serving you well or not, and the reason why.

Table One—Habit Audit. (Example based on Charles Duhigg's work)

Habit	Does it serve me well?	Why/Why not?
Stress/binge eating	No	I feel guilt, out of control, and ashamed
Saying yes instead of no	No	I feel stressed and I sacrifice time I want to spend doing other tasks/activities
Walking my dog	Yes	Fresh air, no technology, time outside with my dog

Once you have established which habits serve you and which ones no longer do, you can get creative and think of new habits you would like to implement into your life. Say, for instance, you love to read but find yourself saying that you don't have the time. Consider your habits: are you looking at your phone on your lunch break? Are you watching hours of TV when you get home from work? Think about your habits and work out which one has a greater meaning—if watching your favourite TV shows means more than reading, then you may want to find another habit to switch reading for. When we become aware of how we are spending our time, we can make informed decisions and changes to our routines.

After doing a habit audit, you likely discovered that there are some habits which no longer serve you well. This takes us to part two of the process—habit switching. Rather than eliminating a habit immediately, habit switching allows you to replace an old habit with something new. You can phase out the habit which no longer serves you and introduce a new one into your routine. On a second table, write down an old habit and the new habit you would like to replace it with and write down a short reason why. This will help you to stay focused when you are trying to implement your new habits.

Table Two—Habit Switching.

Old habit	New habit	Why the switch
Binge eating	Ask if I'm hungry or just bored	To minimise guilt, unnecessary eating, and weight gain
Negative self-talk	Having a positive daily mantra and being kinder to myself	Strengthen my self-compassion
Scrolling through social media during my work breaks	Listening to podcasts	Using my technology for learning rather than as a time filler

If you find it challenging to break a habit, be kind to yourself. Once habits have become automatic or instilled in us, they tend to always be there in our subconscious. Rather than focusing on the habit itself, you could try to focus on the systems in place which facilitated the habit and avoid them.

Here's an example: say you're wanting to break the habit of buying a coffee before work each day. To break the habit, you decide to walk a different way to work to avoid the coffee shop which some days you enter without thought. A few weeks later, you decide to walk down the same street and find yourself with a coffee in hand. And that is how we can fall back into an old habit.

For the data lovers out there, research varies on how long it takes to create a new habit. Some research suggests it can take twenty-one days to create a habit while others suggest it takes sixty-six days or longer. Rather than fixating on a number, try to take each day as it comes and track your progress.

It takes time to create a new habit. Ones that have a positive impact and/or include removing an ingrained habit may take a little while to create. I know when I tried to kick my coffee habit, it wasn't easy. It wasn't until I found a replacement drink (matcha tea and chai lattes) that I was able to kick the habit. My habit of having a warm drink in the morning is still there; I simply changed the beverage. So, if you're feeling a little frustrated or keep falling back into the same old habit, let me ask you this: have you ever found it is easier to create a habit of having say, a takeaway coffee each morning from your local coffee shop than it is to switch a muffin for a piece of fruit during the day? If the answer is yes, be kind to yourself and focus on the progress.

Monitor your progress, and if you miss a day, be kind to yourself. If you miss a day, see it as a chance to reset rather than quit. Do the best with what you have and what you know. If a trigger comes up when you're trying to do a habit switch, take a moment to reflect on what broke the new habit and, most importantly, begin again.

Ask yourself:

1. What habits no longer serve you?
2. What habits do you want to create or strengthen?
3. What habits can you switch?
4. When you're starting to build a new habit, monitor your progress—keep a daily record of the habits.

Chapter 42

THE ART OF MAKING PLANS

Plans don't always unfold the way we hope. When we get attached to the outcome, it can be hard to accept when something doesn't go according to plan. Rather than focusing on the intended outcome, we can change the way we perceive planning. We can use it as a time management tool rather than as a way to try to control the outcome.

Plans are a call to action and they're ever-changing at times. Even the best plans require changes or for a contingency plan to be implemented. Rather than seeing a plan as an absolute, view it as a guide. I like to remind myself that the outcome isn't guaranteed even if you have a plan. I find that the more I try to control the outcome, the less likely it's going to happen.

Planning is an art form and it enables us to build our skills. It strengthens our communication skills, assists with time management, and also empowers you to decide what you want your future to look like. If you like the idea of being in control of most things, it can be easy to get attached to the plan. If you notice that the plan is no longer working, let it go rather than trying to continue on with it. The most critical part of a plan is the planning.

Plans help us give structure to our days. When we make plans with others or just ourselves, we create some certainty. We can schedule time with others and then work out the rest of our day from there. There are some situations when plans get thrown out the window because something unexpected happens and it's during these times that you can either surrender to the situation or try to continue with the plan.

So, you may be thinking, *If a plan doesn't guarantee an outcome I want, why even bother making them*? Plans have their place and they're useful. Just as routines create freedom, plans create a blueprint for the future. Similar to creating an intention, a plan helps you work out how you are going to spend your time and energy. Rather than focusing on the outcome, we can focus on the input.

Creating plans with yourself and others gives you an opportunity to schedule your time. You can use an electronic planner or a journal to plan out your day. Rather than filling your calendar to the brim, try to have breathing room just in case something takes longer or something unexpected happens.

Depending on your life, you may be able to create a similar routine for each day or it may vary. The aim here is to be realistic with how you allocate your time. If you know that a task will take you thirty minutes, allocate this amount of time rather than ten minutes. Take a moment to consider the following aspects of your day:

- **Morning routine:** What time do you usually wake up? What does an ideal morning look like to you? What do you like to achieve before you start your day? Do you exercise or do you have breakfast and run out the door?

- **Your day:** What does your day look like? Are you at work, and if so, do you have meetings or urgent tasks to complete? How do you organise your day (that is, do you have a plan on how you will allocate your time or do you go with the flow?)

- **Afternoon and evening:** What time do you get home? Do you have any appointments? Do you make dinner or exercise? Do you watch a TV show or is this when you'll allocate time to work on your goal? It's important to note that at the end of the day, you should try to do a task that relaxes you. Too often we forget to switch off and end the day. Think of it like this: you are the sunset about to welcome the moon. You put on a beautiful display and allow the sky to turn dark, ready to welcome the day with a beautiful sunrise. Set aside time to relax and, if needed, get ready for the following day.

- **Sleep:** How do you unwind for the day and decompress? What works well and what doesn't? How much sleep do you need to get in order to feel energised the following morning?

Once you begin to plan your day, you can identify how you spend your time. Are you able to follow your schedule with ease? On days where you aren't able to stick to your schedule, identify what is derailing you. If you have a back-to-back schedule, it may be challenging as life often likes to throw in a little spanner whenever we spread ourselves too thin, so if you can, give yourself some breathing room. This will help you feel more in control of your day and if a meeting, task, or situation takes longer than anticipated, you will still have time before moving on to your next task. When you're rushing, you have an increased chance of becoming stressed, frazzled, or less focused and it can be a drain on your energy levels.

When we create a plan for our day, we have an idea of how we are going to spend our time. It's an ideal only; if it doesn't work out exactly as hoped, that's okay. We cannot control every outcome or plan for every unexpected thing. There may be a day that you sleep in late and you feel like you have to play catch up the whole day. In this state, you may feel stressed, rushed, or frazzled. Rather than feeling like you need to still get everything done, see if there is something that can be removed from your plan. Give yourself a break and move it to another day.

Our days don't always go to plan and that's okay. There will be unexpected things that come up and we need to be prepared to let go of what we had planned and go with the flow. It can be easy to be hard on yourself for what wasn't crossed off the list and completed rather than acknowledging what you did achieve. This is when a change in our attitude and mindset is appropriate. Focus on what has been completed rather than not. We can action those items at a later time—if they're not critically important. We have twenty-four hours in a day—we cannot complete our life's work in that time.

Planning is the critical part, and the plan...well, if it works, it works and if not, there's always plan B! Just be sure to find the balance for you. There are under-planners and over-planners and I've fallen into both categories. When I used to plan trips away, I'd research places to visit and plan an itinerary for each day. When it was time to go on the trip, I'd feel time-poor and rushed. If there was a place that sparked an interest but wasn't on the list, I'd ignore the feeling and carry on.

When I took a trip to Tasmania a few years ago, I desperately wanted to see the Lavender Farm in bloom as I'd seen photos online and it looked breathtakingly beautiful. It was a few hours' drive from where I was staying, and when I mentioned it to a tour guide, they said it wasn't worth the trip as the fields weren't in bloom. I drove there anyway and was disappointed. Since then, I've become much more laid back when I'm travelling and as a result, I am more present, more content, and calmer. While planning can be good for giving us direction and a sense of where to focus our time and energy, when followed exactly, it may not always be beneficial. Think of it as an actionable guide rather than a must-do. Things don't always go to plan and that's okay: it's life.

Start off by planning a day, and once you form a habit which suits you, you can move onto other things such as plans on how you intend to achieve your goals.

Chapter 43

ROCKS, PEBBLES, AND SAND

In his book, *First Things First,* Stephen Covey shared an analogy about 'rocks, pebbles, and sand'. This analogy helps us to see how we are allocating our time.[16] The rocks symbolise our important items such as our non-negotiables, family, friendships, goals, and bucket list items. Pebbles symbolise the things we enjoy doing but may not be as fulfilling as our rocks, such as watching television or browsing social media platforms. That leads us to sand, which symbolises the mundane tasks such as chores, running errands, and so forth.

Typically, we fill up our glasses (schedule) with sand and pebbles before making room for our rocks. When you say yes to something else, such as a pebble, or you fill your glass with sand, there won't be space (or time) for your rocks.

Pebbles and sand are time-consuming, and for most of us, they fill up the majority of our glasses. They could be the frivolous tasks we commit to when we have no interest, or the ways we spend our time (such as browsing social media platforms for longer than anticipated). While it may not be possible to fill every day with just rocks, it is worthwhile reflecting on what fills your glass currently and if you feel that it works for you.

Go-getters fill their glass with rocks, and from there they choose what they want to prioritise. Putting others before yourself and your ambitions may seem selfless; however, it means you are allowing others to write your story. Try to regain control of your time by placing more rocks in the glass. This will help you get back into the driver's seat. To take better care of others, we must learn how to take care of ourselves. When we neglect ourselves, we can become bitter, resentful, and in turn hurt those we treasure. You can do anything but not everything. Time is finite and those we idolise for their successes often have daily habits and time management skills that allow them to prioritise what needs to get done so they can achieve their goals, day in, day out.

Some claim to be time-poor, but regardless of who we are, our title, or the amount of money in our bank account, we each have the same number of seconds, minutes, and hours in a day. What differentiates each of us is how we use our time. When you place a high value on time and know how much your time is worth, then you can begin to use it more efficiently. That doesn't necessarily mean that you need to fill each minute of the day; however, you may want to do a time audit to see where you can gain time. Does the meeting need to go ahead and if so, how much time will it really take? Can you ask your employer if you can work from home or another location a few times each week to save you the commute? With your personal life, what changes can you make to spend time on passion projects, hobbies, or on the things which are of high value to you? For instance, if you want to spend more time reading books, reaching for a television remote won't help.

Steve Jobs said, 'Deciding what not to do is as important as deciding what to do.' We have limited time; we may as well make the most of it and that begins with rocks. Find your balance. It isn't selfish to focus on your own goals. It is your life—you get to decide what your priorities are.

Don't be afraid of scheduling your time. When you put something on the schedule, hold yourself accountable and see it through. Rather than filling your schedule to the brim, try to keep a buffer zone. Think of it as your emergency time. As much as we want life to run to our schedule, chances are things may not go to plan or unexpected tasks may come up. When we leave space to allow for the unexpected things, we can be proactive rather than flustered and reactive.

If you have experienced the stress that comes with waking up later than planned or having to rush around, it's often challenging to reclaim the day when you wake up in this state. The day seems to get ahead of you and your energy is focused on reclaiming your time rather than focusing on what's ahead. To give yourself the best chance at owning your day, schedule your rocks, focus on your daily priorities, and repeat. Add your rocks first and then fill your schedule from there. Make your non-negotiables your priority. When you value your time rather than removing rocks to make room for more sand and pebbles, you can achieve more. When we compromise and set aside our non-negotiables, a habit may form. Your rocks matter; they're your foundation. Remember, self-care and valuing what is important to you is not frivolous or selfish, it's necessary.

By focusing your time, you can begin to achieve tasks. You can do this by allocating your time. If your mind wanders onto other tasks or you feel tempted to multitask, take a moment to refocus and tell yourself the following: 'This time is for __ and I will focus on ___ until it is completed.'

Ask yourself:

Draw a cup and try to determine your rock to sand and pebble ratio. You can draw two cups: one for your work week and one for your weekends. Next, draw your ideal cup/s and compare it to your current cup/s. Alternatively, you can write a list.

1. What are your rocks?
2. What are your pebbles?
3. What is your sand?
4. What changes can you make in the short, medium, and long term?
5. How will these changes impact your life?

Chapter 44

INTIMATE RELATIONSHIPS

Take a moment to reflect on a time when you have felt like you have been taken for granted. Chances are you didn't feel too great. Negative emotions may have risen to the surface and you may have begun to tally up in your mind the things you did for them and what they didn't do for you. You began to give less to the relationship, hoping that they will notice what you did before and show appreciation.

I have tried this, and it doesn't work. Acting in a passive aggressive manner doesn't solve the problem. Usually, the other person doesn't notice or if they do, they're not sure what the reason is for your change in behaviour. It's harder to sit down and talk about it, but it resolves the issue quicker. If it's a blind spot, they may not even be aware of how they're making you feel, and chances are it's not intentional. Let the other person know and then it's their choice to respond or resolve it moving forward. Rather than attack them, explain the situation from your perspective and how it made you feel.

I'll use a personal example to illustrate this. There are times when I feel like I am doing most of the housework and I get frustrated. I could be passive aggressive, or I could talk to Jesse about it. I could yell at him and say something like, 'You never do anything to help out around the house; I'm always the one who's responsible for keeping the house looking tidy,' which won't result in a good conversation, or I could say, 'I appreciate all that you do around the house but at the moment, I am feeling a little overwhelmed with my share of the housework. Would you mind helping out with [insert chore here]?' The best way to resolve a situation is to talk about it and clear the air. In this instance, Jesse may not have realised how I felt; from there, we can work out a plan.

Let's talk about intimacy for a moment. Intimacy is more than a physical connection. It's about the depth of a bond between two people and the moments shared. It's about trust and vulnerability and the ability to be seen and heard—and to see and hear another person—without judgement. It's about taking off the armour and allowing another to see you for all that you are.

Just as we have our own love language, we also have different definitions of what intimacy is and looks like. As I have discovered, Jesse and I have different ideas of what intimacy is, so I'd encourage you to think of what it means to you and then ask your partner to see if there are any similarities or differences. Instead of being upset at how you are treated compared to what you expect, communicate and learn from each other. As a woman, my idea of intimacy includes having deep and meaningful conversations, sharing moments, and being close to one another. On the flip side, Jesse tells me that he is happy just being in the same room as me, even if we are each doing on our thing. Earlier in our relationship, I thought we were drifting apart because we weren't being as intimate as we had been, according to my definition, but because his definition was different, he wasn't concerned.

Admittedly, he had to say this a few times before I really heard and understood that he was trying to be intimate. He didn't see any problems because we were still spending time together and, for him, that is intimate. It was just in a different way to me and what I was expecting. Since that day, I have made a conscious choice to change my behaviour as I was able to see it from his perspective. Rather than thinking he was being distant or not wanting to be close to me, I now see it from his point of view, and I value the times when he is being intimate by his own definition.

If you want to build stronger relationships and improve intimacy, take time to learn what intimacy means to you and the person you are wanting to be closer to. It may avoid a breakdown in communication or drifting apart if it isn't addressed. Explain what intimacy means to you and listen to your partner's definition and go from there.

Another way to build a strong relationship is to celebrate the milestones. My current relationship is the first long-term relationship I have been in. So, each year on our anniversary, I like to celebrate. Whether it's a road trip, a dinner at a favourite restaurant, or a shared experience, I like to mark the day. I'm the same when it comes to birthdays and other days where you have the ability to show your appreciation of someone else. It reminds them how special you believe that they are and that you notice what they do.

It's easy to overlook the seemingly small things such as doing the dishes, taking out the garbage, walking the dog, or mowing the lawn, but many times, others do those tasks to help you out and vice versa. Most of us don't come home thinking about how excited we are to take out the rubbish (especially in the middle of winter or when it's raining) but we know it will help out our loved one, so we do it regardless. If you notice your loved one doing this, say thank you and show your appreciation. If it's a chore that your loved one usually does, you could surprise them by doing it instead.

It's easy to compete and claim you do more than they do (and maybe that's true) but saying thank you still goes a long way. We all like to be appreciated, and when you're around people for long periods of time, it can be tempting to settle into a routine and assume that they will always do the task or take them for granted. When we take someone for granted, it can have negative impacts. However, if we break out of the 'granted bubble', we can reconnect. It's not a competition; it's about working as a team and walking through life together.

Ask yourself:

1. What does intimacy mean to you?
2. How does your loved one define and show intimacy?
3. Notice a small thing that your loved one does and say thank you.

Chapter 45

RELATIONSHIPS—WHO WE SURROUND OURSELVES WITH MATTERS

Who you surround yourself with matters. They can either lift you up or bring you down. Relationships are vital to our health and wellbeing, but when we are surrounded by those who drain of us our energy, we cannot be our best selves. While it is easier said than done, it's crucial that you create and nurture healthy relationships and free yourself of toxic people. Once you are able to free yourself of the toxic relationships, you feel lighter.

We may not even realise that we have toxic relationships at first. We may grow accustomed to the way we feel around certain people and consider it normal. When I was in my early twenties, I had a few girlfriends who were fun and lively, but they didn't make me feel good after a while. From negative remarks on how I looked in certain outfits to having to justify why I wasn't able to stop working on an assignment to go out clubbing last minute, it grew tiring after a while. There was also an influx of drama attached, and once I realised that the friendships weren't serving me well and I wasn't able to be the friend they wanted, I decided to let it go. I did have a conversation first about how I felt but the situation didn't improve.

Relationships are not there to make you feel lousy about yourself. If you constantly feel like you have to justify what you are doing, the goals you have, or who you authentically are, it may be time to have a heart-to-heart with the person and explain how their behaviour is making you feel. When others drain you of your energy, you feel exhausted, but when you're surrounded by those who lift you up and inspire you, the dynamic is much more positive. Consider whether you want to lift your spirits and be emotionally drained. You have the power to choose who is in your life. In the words of Jim Rohn, 'you are the average of the five people you spend the most time with.' So, who do you want to be?

Not everyone is meant to be in your life permanently. Some are meant to be there for a few chapters while others, such as a life partner, children, or family, stay for a while longer. Rather than holding on to a relationship that no longer serves either of you, be brave enough to let it go. Whether it's a romantic relationship or friendship, it hurts to let it go, but think of what you will be gaining. No-one can take away the memories made but it frees you both up to create a different future—one more in line with what you want. It's okay to value the history you have with someone but don't let it be the reason you're holding onto something longer than you should. When you're staying in a relationship because it's convenient, it's time to reflect on whether it's something you want to improve or let go of. You don't need to invest more of your life in a relationship if you know that it truly isn't serving you anymore.

Whether it's a friendship, family member, or romantic relationship, it is never easy to let go. When I have had to end a relationship or friendship, I try to not place blame on the other person. Instead, I try to explain how I feel and that some space may be needed or that it's no longer working. Sometimes you are both moving in different directions. It's not an easy conversation to have, but once it's over, you feel lighter. It's as much allowing the other person to move on and create space for relationships which light them up as it is for you. You—and the other person—deserve to be happy, safe, and at peace with yourself rather than being a shadow of yourself. Be brave enough to let someone go when they're no longer right for you. Accept when a chapter is over.

You have the power to walk away. There is a way out. You are not alone, no matter how you feel. Know that you are a beautiful soul with endless power, strength, and resilience and you deserve to be treated with respect and dignity. If an individual or group are belittling you, be assertive and remove yourself from the situation. The longer you stay, the more challenging it may seem to leave. Rather than thinking you're the problem, focus on your self-worth and remind yourself that you are leaving because you love yourself and want to live a life not ruled by fear or self-hate, or in a state of invisibility. You are strong and deserve to be surrounded by people who really see you, encourage you, and uplift you. If you are willing to be this person to others, you will attract the sameness into your life. Just have faith. Live your life from a place of love and kindness rather than fear and resentment.

Depending on your situation, you may want to turn to someone who you trust or reach out to an organisation who can help you leave a dangerous situation. Know that you are brave for doing so and trust the process. Whether it's a destructive relationship or friendship, know you are worth more than you feel at the moment. Walking away takes courage and some toxic relationships are more challenging to leave than others. If you are able to walk away, trust that you will be making space for better relationships.

You cannot succeed when you're surrounded by those who don't believe in you or your dreams. You'll spend energy justifying your decisions, and their lack of confidence in yourself will cause you to question yourself and your path. It's tiring and, to be frank, a waste of your time and energy. Relationships are give and take. Each has its own status quo, and while it may sway out of balance every so often, it's critical that it returns to the status quo at some point. If you find you're giving more than you're receiving or vice versa, have an open conversation with the other person to see if you can find a resolution rather than being resented or resentful. If the relationship cannot be repaired, consider whether it is time to let go. Picture your life in three, five, and ten years' time. Do you see that person in your life?

We have had relationships that we know aren't healthy for us to sustain, but we don't allow ourselves to move on. Whether it's a friendship, platonic relationship, or intimate relationship, if it's draining you of your time, energy, and happiness, it may be time to let it go. I'm not suggesting that you break up with your significant other, divorce your parents or siblings, or ghost your friends, but if this chapter resonates with you and a person comes to mind, then you may want to do a relationship audit to see if they still deserve to be in your life and vice versa.

You may also want to think about yourself. How do you treat your friends, family, and significant other? Are there changes that you can make to improve the relationship? If you're ready to receive feedback, consider asking those you treasure for constructive ways to enhance your relationship with them. You may even want to read Gary Chapman's book *The Five Love Languages* to see if you can identify your love language and that of your closest companions if you don't feel comfortable asking for feedback just yet.[17] I found this to be an insightful book to read because it taught me that we can each feel loved in a different way and that's okay. If you are seeking feedback or having a conversation with another, be gentle and accept that you cannot force someone else to change. It's hard enough to change ourselves, as we know.

I believe we all need people around who truly know us and are willing to celebrate our successes and be there when you need help, as well as those who can keep us on track and help us to refocus when we aren't quite ourselves.

In order to thrive, we need to feel a sense of belonging because, at our core, we are social beings. If we look at Maslow's hierarchy of needs, belonging is a lower-order need, and if we want to attain our higher-order needs, the lower-order needs require fulfilment first.[18] If we feel isolated and are trying to make it on our own, the journey can be isolating and lonely, and our spirit will be drained.

With that in mind, you can have different relationships with people in your tribe. Some may be coaches or mentors that are helping you build a specific skill or habit while another person may be the one you go to when you need a pep talk, and so forth. Just like friendships, these individuals can be there for you in one or a number of ways. We cannot be everything to everyone. Even trying to be a complete all-in-one package to someone may not be possible either, and vice versa.

Cultivate relationships that uplift you. Free yourself from toxic friendships or relationships that no longer serve you. Life is too short to surround yourself with those who are not meant to be in your life anymore. Fear will inevitably creep in and tell you to hold on, to fight for it, and that you're being unreasonable. Only you know, in your heart of hearts, when it's time to move on, and if it's time, let it go and walk away. You will have the memories of your time together and it's okay to grieve. When you lose someone who you care for deeply, it hurts to say goodbye, but you just need to remind yourself that it's for the best and keep moving forward.

Ask yourself:

1. What gestures make you feel loved?
2. Reflect on your closest friendships and relationships—what makes them special?
3. Are there people in your life who you may need to put some space between?
4. Are there people who you may want to ask for feedback from?
5. Are you proud of the person you are to others (such as a partner, parent, child, friend)? Why/why not?

CONCLUSION

I've retyped this chapter multiple times because I'm at a loss for words. I don't want to sign off with a cliché, nor do I feel the desire to summarise what you've just read.

I can only hope to impart one piece of advice which is this: we are all human. We get to choose whether we want to be a human being or human doing. We can race through our lives at a fast pace or we can choose to slow it down and enjoy the day as it unfolds. Life isn't going to be perfect; it doesn't owe us anything, but *we* owe it *ourselves* to learn about ourselves—the things that make us unique and fill our hearts with joy and the skills we can offer those around us.

Writing this book has been my way of unpacking what I have learnt about myself and self-development to date. I still have days where I feel as though I'm not making any progress towards my goals, but then I look back and remember what I have done.

We are all constantly evolving, and while we may not control our future entirely, we can choose certain parts. We can choose to put our phones down and be present in the company of others. We can choose to become more aware of how we use our time and whether it aligns with our values. We can choose to make our dreams a reality.

If you told me a few years ago that I would write a book (back when I only had a vague dream of writing a book someday), I would have laughed. It seemed unlikely, like a dream that wasn't going to be any more than that. But here we are. The point is, we can do it, if we choose to.

ABOUT THE AUTHOR

Tash Jarvis is a self-development enthusiast. Drawing on the lessons she has learnt on her journey to date, Tash has authored her first book *From Human Being to Human Doing*.

She lives in Perth, Western Australia with her fiancé, Jesse, and their furbaby Lana.

For more information, you can connect with Tash on Instagram @tash_jarvis or read her posts at <www.becoming yourultimateself.com>.

REFERENCES

1. Jon Acuff, *Quitter: Closing the gap between your day job and your dream job.* Ramsey Press, 2015.

2. Dr Joe Dispenza, *Breaking the Habit of Being Yourself. How to lose your mind and create a new one.* Hay House, 2012.

3. Voltaire, La Bégueule: Conte Morale. Originally published 1772.

4. Hal Elrod, *The Miracle Morning: The 6 habits that will transform your life before 8am.* John Murray Learning, 2018.

5. Rosenman, R. H., Brand, R. J., Sholtz, R. I., & Friedman, M. Multivariate prediction of coronary heart disease during 8.5 year follow-up in the Western Collaborative Group Study. *The American Journal of Cardiology, 37(6),* 903-910. 1976.

6. Michael F Kay, *Seeing the World Through Your Lens: What you believe becomes your reality.* Psychology Today, September 18, 2012. Retrieved on February 15, 2021 https://www.psychologytoday.com/au/blog/financial-life-focus/201209/seeing-the-world-through-your-lens

7. Catherine Moore, *What is the Negativity Bias and How Can it be Overcome?* Positive Psychology.com January 9, 2020. Retrieved on February 15, 2021 https://positivepsychology.com/3-steps-negativity-bias/

8. Kyle Benson, *The Magic Relationship Ration, According to Science.* The Gottman Institute, October 4, 2017. Retrieved from https://www.gottman.com/blog/the-magic-relationship-ratio-according-science/ on February 15, 2021.

9 Randy Pausch, *The Last Lecture*. Hachette Books, 2008.

10 Abraham Maslow, *A theory of Human Motivation*. Psychological Review, 50 (4): 370-96 1943.

11 Dispenza (see 2)

12 *What are the 5 Stages of Burnout?* Thisiscalmer.com August 20,2020. Retrieved on February 15, 2021 https://www.thisiscalmer.com/blog/5-stages-of-burnout;

13 *Oprah's SuperSoul Conversations Podcast – Brene Brown: Rising Strong.* YouTube July 18, 2018. Retrieved from https://www.youtube.com/watch?v=DMZvKHO_nb8 on February 15, 2021.

14 M Szegedy-Maszak, 'Mysteries of the mind', *USNews*, U.S. News & World Report L.P., 28 Feb 2005, retrieved via archive.org Feb 2021, https://web.archive.org/web/20050301001555/http://www.usnews.com/usnews/issue/050228/health/28think.htm.

15 Charles Duhigg, *The Power of Habit: Why we do what we do in life and business*. Random House, 2012.

16 Stephen Covey, A Roger Merrill and Rebecca R Merrill, *First Things First: To live, to love, to learn, to leave a legacy*. Simon and Schuster, 1994.

17 Gary Chapman, *The Five Love Languages: How to express heartfelt commitment to your mate*. Northfield Publishing, 1992.

18 Maslow (see 10)

CPSIA information can be obtained
at www.ICGtesting.com
Printed in the USA
BVHW031656081122
651457BV00014B/445